EVENTS & OUTCOMES
THE
REFORMATION

FIONA MACDONALD

RAINTREE
STECK-VAUGHN
PUBLISHERS

A Harcourt Company

Austin   New York
www.raintreesteckvaughn.com

Edited by Rachel Norridge
Designed by Neil Sayer
Maps by Tim Smith

Acknowledgments

Cover image The Bridgeman Art Library **background image** the art archive **p. 6** The Bridgeman Art Library **p. 7** (top) the art archive (bottom) The Bridgeman Art Library **p. 8** the art archive **p. 9** (top) The Bridgeman Art Library (bottom) The Bridgeman Art Library **p. 10** the art archive **p. 11** (top) The Bridgeman Art Library (bottom) The Bridgeman Art Library **p. 12** The Bridgeman Art Library **p. 13** (top) Mary Evans (bottom) the art archive **p. 14** the art archive **p. 15** The Bridgeman Art Library **p. 16** the art archive **p. 17** (top) the art archive (bottom) The Bridgeman Art Library **p. 18** (top) the art archive (bottom) the art archive **p. 19** Mary Evans Picture Library **p. 20** (top) The Bridgeman Art Library (bottom) The Bridgeman Art Library **p. 21** The Bridgeman Art Library **p. 22** (top) Mary Evans Picture Library (bottom) The Bridgeman Art Library **p. 23** The Bridgeman Art Library **p. 25** the art archive **p. 26** the art archive **p. 27** (top) The Bridgeman Art Library (bottom) The Bridgeman Art Library **p. 28** (top) The Bridgeman Art Library (bottom) Mary Evans Picture Library **p. 29** Mary Evans Picture Library **p. 30** the art archive **p. 31** (left) The Bridgeman Art Library (right) The Bridgeman Art Library **p. 33** Mary Evans Picture Library **p. 34** The Bridgeman Art Library **p. 35** the art archive **p. 37** the art archive **p. 39** (left) the art archive (right) The Bridgeman Art Library **p. 40** the art archive **p. 41** Topham Picturepoint **p. 42** The Bridgeman Art Library **p. 43** The Bridgeman Art Library **p. 44** (top) Mary Evans Picture Library (bottom) the art archive **p. 45** The Bridgeman Art Library **p. 46** The Bridgeman Art Library **p. 47** The Bridgeman Art Library **p. 48** Topham Picturepoint **p. 49** (top) Topham Picturepoint (bottom) Corbis **p. 51** The Bridgeman Art Library **p. 52** the art archive **p. 53** (top) The Bridgeman Art Library (bottom) Mary Evans Picture Library **p. 55** Topham Picturepoint **p. 56** (top left) the art archive (top right) The Bridgeman Art Library **p. 57** The Bridgeman Art Library **p. 58** Mary Evans Picture Library **p. 59** (top) The Bridgeman Art Library (bottom) Mary Evans Picture Library **p. 60** The Bridgeman Art Library **p. 61** (top) Mary Evans Picture Library (bottom) Mary Evans Picture Library **p. 63** (top) the art archive (bottom) Mary Evans Picture Library **p. 64** Mary Evans Picture Library **p. 65** Topham Picturepoint **p. 66** Topham Picturepoint **p. 67** Topham Picturepoint **p. 68** The Bridgeman Art Library **p. 69** (top) Topham Picturepoint (bottom) Topham Picturepoint **p. 70** The Bridgeman Art Library **p. 71** Topham Picturepoint **p. 72** Topham Picturepoint

CONTENTS

INTRODUCTION

What Is Christianity?

Christians believe that Jesus Christ was the son of God born in Bethlehem (now on the West Bank of Palestine), about 2,000 years ago. Christ preached about peace and justice and healed many people who were considered incurable. Hanged on a cross near Jerusalem, he arose three days later, appearing to some of his apostles and declaring that he would return at the world's end. Christianity spread rapidly throughout the Mediterranean region, developing into a major world religion.

Power and Politics

Over the next ten centuries the Christian Church became a large, international organization, with a hierarchy of officials (deacons, priests, bishops, and archbishops), vast territorial possessions, and great riches—thanks to gifts of land and treasure from Christian people. It ran many fine schools, colleges, libraries, and other centers of learning, and provided a literate, well-educated, all-male elite that led many secular governments, as well as administering the Church's own complex bureaucracy. (Until 1500, or even later, most ordinary people could not read or write.) Church leaders, headed by the Pope, played an important part in local and national politics. Many became government ministers or advisors to kings and nobles. Often they were related to the people they advised, since wealthy families encouraged at least one of their children to make a career in the Church. This brought them influence and prestige—as well as (they hoped) closer links with God.

All Souls College, Oxford, and its founders and benefactors. Devout Christians donated money to build colleges such as this, as well as churches and hospitals.

Private Lives

By 1000 the Church influenced all aspects of life in most parts of Europe. Christian lands were divided into

6

Pope Leo X (1475–1521) with two of his cardinals. People criticized the popes' power, but still valued the Church.

parishes (covering one or two villages), each with its own church and priest, or priests. In England, for example, there were almost 10,000 parish churches by 1500. All important rites of passage, from infant baptism to burial, were marked by Christian sacraments. Christian festivals celebrated important community events, such as plowing the fields or gathering the harvest. Church courts regulated intimate aspects of people's private lives, and had the power to punish them for breaking Church rules. Today, many of these Christian traditions still survive, but they are frequently considered as somewhat outmoded. But for medieval people, the Church's ritual code provided mechanisms for coping with the insecurities of life and finding comfort despite them. As one historian notes, these rituals also provided:

 rites and entertainments that gave medieval life its rhythm and color.

The Supernatural

"The Last Judgment" (c.1450) by Stephan Lochner is a powerful image of souls being judged by God. Such images portrayed familiar Christian hopes and fears.

Most important of all, the Church offered a framework of beliefs linking humanity to a divine, superhuman power. The Church also held the key to a glorious—or terrible—fate after death. By enacting its rituals of the sacraments, it contained and conveyed virtue, and was the only legitimate source of spiritual power. Priests taught that:

 outside the Church, there is no salvation.

These transcendent beliefs fit in with earlier, pre-Christian ideas and superstitions, which many Christian people still believed in. They saw the world as haunted by countless invisible spirits with the power to help or harm, who had to be appeased by carefully performed rituals or sacrifices. Almost everyone believed in magic, witchcraft, ghosts, curses, and charms.

Calls for Reform

The Christian Church was not always peaceful or united, and it frequently provoked fierce criticism for its extravagance, pride (both worldly and spiritual), and political ambitions. In this book we will explore one episode when critics of the Church, calling for reform, initiated a long process of social, political, and religious change. Historians call this process the Reformation. It began around 1500, but its effects can still be felt today. Some historians prefer to talk about several Reformations instead of a single Reformation. They argue that the process lasted for so long, took so many different forms, changed direction so many times, and became so closely linked with national and international politics, that it is wrong to think of it as a unified movement with one single, simple religious aim.

Wider Perspectives

It is important to remember that the Reformation began at a time when life in Europe was changing rapidly in many ways. From around 1400, sailors from Portugal pioneered new sea routes along the west coast of Africa toward the Indian Ocean. In 1492 Christopher Columbus, financed by Portugal's great rival, Spain, sailed across the Atlantic to reach America—and astonished all Europe with his descriptions of a "new world." In northern Europe, citizens of commercial towns grew rich through trade and by providing financial services—unlike most Europeans who earned their living from the land. Some German towns became centers of new technology, producing deadly weapons from iron, such as the cannon. The first European printing press with movable type was also invented in Germany, by Johannes Gutenberg, around 1450.

At the same time, the cities of southern Europe, especially in Italy, were home to a revolutionary new movement in art, scholarship, and ideas that eventually spread throughout Europe. Known as the Renaissance (rebirth), it was inspired by the excavation of many Greek and Roman buildings and works of art, and by the rediscovery of ancient, pre-Christian, Greek and Roman learning that had been lost to most of Europe after Roman power collapsed around 500. This knowledge had been carefully preserved, however, by many Muslim scholars as well as in some remote Christian monasteries.

Christopher Columbus set sail on his historic voyage across the Atlantic Ocean in August 1492. Exploration and growing international trade ushered in a period of great change.

This design for an ideal city, imagined by 15th-century Italian Renaissance artist Piero della Francesca, was based on Greek and Roman ruins.

When this knowledge became available again, after around 1300, it encouraged whole new areas of learning, especially in science, philosophy, and the understanding of ancient texts—including early versions of the Bible. Renaissance scholars became known as humanists, since, like the pagan Greeks and Romans, they shared an enthusiasm for the dignity of human values in place of religious dogma. Although most humanists did not set out directly to challenge Christian teachings, humanist ideas had profoundly unsettling implications. If, as the ancient Greeks had believed, man was the measure of all things, where did that leave God and the Church?

Questions and Challenges

These changes did not cause the Reformation, but they did help to create a climate of questioning and uncertainty that may have encouraged critics of the Church to challenge some of its ideas. The amazing news brought back by explorers of distant places made some people look at European traditions (including Christianity) in a critical way. Scientists like astronomer Nicolaus Copernicus (1473–1543), compared their own experiments and observations with Church teachings, and suggested that the Church was wrong. Literary scholars began to prepare new, improved translations of the Bible, hoping to get closer to the truths they believed it contained. Although printed books were very expensive (and most people could not read them), the new invention of printing became an important way of spreading Reformation questions and ideas.

Movable type, first used in presses in Germany, enabled books to be produced more quickly and cheaply than ever before.

PART I: SETTING THE SCENE

CALLS FOR CHANGE

One Faith, One Church?

From the earliest years of the Christian Church, there were fierce disagreements over doctrine. These, combined with bitter national and international political disputes and contrasting local customs, meant that Christians did not always agree on how the Church should be run. As a result, many separate Churches developed, in Europe, Central Asia, North Africa, Russia, and the Middle East. The European Church—also known as the Catholic Church—had been founded by St. Peter (died 64 A.D.) and was headed by his successors, the popes (bishops of Rome). In 1054 it split in two. While Christians in Western Europe remained members of the Catholic Church, loyal to the Pope, Christians in Eastern Europe joined the Orthodox Church, based in Constantinople (now Istanbul).

The Pope claimed spiritual authority over all Christians in West European lands. There was no alternative Church organization, and no rival religious leader. There were, however, several different ways of Christian living approved by the Church, and many ways of worshiping. Occasionally, rebellious priests, dissenting scholars, or maverick local holy men or women, with new (and sometimes bizarre) ideas about Christianity, tried to set up religious organizations of their own, but they were labeled heretics and vigorously persecuted by Church officials.

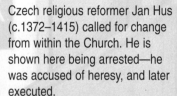

Czech religious reformer Jan Hus (c.1372–1415) called for change from within the Church. He is shown here being arrested—he was accused of heresy, and later executed.

Back to Basics

This stern attitude toward heretics did not mean there was no diversity within the Church. There were constant calls for spiritual renewal among Christians and for changes to the Catholic Church's own organization. Usually these demanded that the Church go back to basics and that priests and people should live pure, holy lives, as the first Christians had done. For example, St. Francis of Assisi (c.1182–1226) and St. Dominic (c.1170–1221) founded two new orders of friars— priests who aimed to live simply in the community, preaching the Christian message and encouraging charity toward the sick and the poor.

Although strictly conformist in doctrine, the friars represented a potential threat to the organizational unity of the medieval Church and its power to impose discipline. Unlike monks and nuns who lived shut away from the rest of the world, or priests who were subject to regular inspection by bishops, friars were free agents. They vowed obedience to the head of their order, but he could not monitor them closely.

John Wycliffe's calls for reform were tolerated, until he attacked the mass—the Church's most important and most respected ritual.

Bibles and Private Prayer

In England, a university teacher named John Wycliffe (c.1329–1384) made more radical doctrinal demands. Like St. Francis and St. Dominic, he called for priests and Church leaders to spend more time on spiritual duties and less on worldly matters, such as politics, church finances, and the law. He also questioned some of the Church's key teachings. In particular, he argued that ordinary Christian people ought to be able to seek God's truth by themselves, without the help of priests or elaborate Church rituals. This was a fundamental attack on the Church's role, and on the exalted position of priests as sole providers of God's truth. Wycliffe also argued that Christians should be allowed to read the Bible in their own language (he prepared its first translation into English). At that time, the Bible was only available in Latin—the ancient, official language of the Catholic Church.

A romanticized 19th-century image of Lollards meeting to read the Bible and discuss religious ideas.

Wycliffe was forced to retire. After his death, his followers, known as Lollards, continued to develop his ideas even though they risked being charged with heresy. They criticized many popular religious customs, such as worshiping the relics of saints, declaring that they were more like witchcraft than true Christianity. But in 1401 the government in England passed the first law allowing heretics to be burned. The Lollards were forced into hiding, but they continued to hold secret meetings for prayer and Bible study, and their religious ideas survived for the next 100 years.

Reform from Within

The Lollards, and other groups like them, challenged Catholic teaching. But there were also demands for reform from loyal Catholic scholars and Church officials who wanted to return the Church to a purer, simpler state. From 1274 onward, they organized meetings—called Councils of Church leaders—demanding that the Catholic Church be reformed "in head and limbs."

Public Duties

That was easier said than done. The Church was too large and complex an organization to accept rapid, far-reaching change. Moreover, many senior Churchmen stood to lose too much. Popes and cardinals ranked as "princes of the Church" and did not want to give up that prestige. Many were expert scholars, lawyers, and administrators, and the Church was their career. Church leaders had also become deeply involved in politics—sometimes scandalously so. For example, in 1305 Pope Clement V, after political quarrels in Italy, moved from the popes' traditional home in Rome to the French city of Avignon. Six more popes lived there until 1377. Then, between 1378 and 1417, supporters within the Church of warring French and Italian rulers elected two rival popes.

Each senior Churchman jealously guarded the

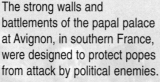

The strong walls and battlements of the papal palace at Avignon, in southern France, were designed to protect popes from attack by political enemies.

traditional privileges attached to his position—or positions, since many held more than one well-paid job. They eagerly defended their rights to appoint priests and other Church officials (for which they often charged a fee), to collect taxes, and to hold law courts, since all were great sources of wealth. However, many Church leaders were less enthusiastic about carrying out their religious duties, such as training priests, inspecting monasteries and nunneries, and visiting parishes to check on the spiritual welfare of ordinary men and women.

Private Vices

From around the 11th century, all Catholic priests were forbidden to marry and had to remain celibate. But some Church leaders lived openly with mistresses, and fathered children whom they often married into powerful noble families or appointed to senior jobs in the Church. Many parishioners did not object to priests marrying and having children, but they did expect fidelity. Most were horrified by Alexander VI (pope from 1431–1503), who was reported to have given:

a supper to the cardinals and grandees of his court, placing at each side of his guests two courtesans (prostitutes), whose only dress consisted of a loose garment of gauze and garlands of flowers... when the meal was over, those women...performed dances—at first alone, afterwards with the guests. At a signal...the garments of the women fell down and the dance went on, to the applause of His Holiness.

A Warning Voice

Church leaders, priests, and ordinary people were appalled by Alexander's behavior. Some encouraged measures to purify their own small corner of the Church, such as improved training programs for priests, and the publication of prayer books and spiritual handbooks for lay people. Some people joined religious guilds and gave to Christian charities. Others became involved in movements to encourage good, Christian citizenship. The largest, and most famous, of these was led by friar Girolamo Savonarola (1452–1498). He urged rulers of the city of Florence, Italy, to set up a Christian republic with strict laws warning against vice and vanities. But because Savonarola refused to accept orders from the Pope, he was accused of heresy, and executed.

This savage cartoon from 1540 attacks immoral popes and senior Churchmen by showing them seated at the "table of vice."

A stern portrait of reforming friar Girolamo Savonarola.

Essential Truths

While many people criticized the corruption and inefficiency of the Catholic Church, this did not stop them from being loyal believers. They still accepted the Church's religious teachings. What were these teachings? Like all Christian organizations, the Catholic Church declared that Jesus was the son of God. It also maintained that, after his execution, Jesus had come back to life, then gone to join God in heaven. Soon afterward, God had sent the Holy Spirit to guide all Christian people. God the Father, Jesus the Son, and the Holy Spirit were seen as three parts of one single God, and were called the Trinity.

The Church recognized that life on Earth was often "a vale of tears," full of pain and injustice, to be endured with patience and resignation to God's will. But Christians were encouraged to hope for a better life after death. This was, however, only available to those who had been saved from sin. According to the Church, there were two kinds of sin, and everyone, even a newborn baby, was guilty of the first kind. This was original sin, and it was shared by all humanity. It had polluted the world ever since Adam and Eve had disobeyed God. Most people were guilty of personal sins, as well. These were committed whenever a man or woman broke God's moral laws, summarized in the Ten Commandments and in Jesus' instruction to love your neighbor as yourself.

This altar painting by Flemish artist Rogier van der Weyden (1400–1464) shows the seven sacraments that saved Christian souls from sin, alongside a scene of Christ's crucifixion.

Saved by Sacraments

The Church claimed that it could save people from sin through its sacraments (rituals for salvation). This ritual purification from sin was the Church's main purpose, and the spiritual reason for its power. There were seven sacraments, and they could be performed only by priests. Five took place just once—baptism, confirmation, marriage, ordination (becoming a priest), and extreme unction (blessing the dying). But two sacraments needed to be repeated throughout a Christian's life. These were confession of sins to a priest followed by penance, and taking part in the Church's most holy act of worship, called mass.

Confession and penance wiped out any personal sins committed since the last time a Christian had confessed. Mass removed original sin, as well. During mass, worshipers remembered the last meal that Jesus had shared with his followers, and also his bloody death. According to the Church, that sacrifice of Jesus' life had washed away original sin. During mass, priests blessed special bread and wine and shared the bread with worshipers. The Church taught that Jesus became mysteriously present, and that the bread and wine were transubstantiated (transformed) into his actual flesh and blood. His sacrifice was repeated, as was the removal of original sin.

Medieval Christian artists honored the sacrament of mass in mystical images like this one from 16th-century Germany, called "The Miracle of Transubstantiation."

Doctrinal Differences

The precise meaning of the sacraments had been discussed in detail, but never seriously doubted, by Catholic scholars for hundreds of years. However, during the 15th century, some began to challenge the Church's teachings about salvation. In particular, they questioned the need for sacraments to be conducted by priests, the power of penance and good works to cancel personal sin, and the mystery of transubstantiation. They also emphasized the existing idea that it was not enough for worshipers simply to take part in the sacraments— they must have genuine faith and God-given grace.

Safe and Straightforward?

What did Christianity mean to most people in Western Europe around 1500? In many ways, belonging to the Church seemed comforting, safe, and straightforward. If Christians took part in the Church's sacraments, paid Church taxes, and obeyed Church laws, they had a reasonable chance of enjoying life after death in heaven.

Penance and Purgatory

To many people, the sacrament of penance was most important, because it pardoned their sins. To purchase further pardons, they gave generously to charities, funded new chantry chapels, and paid for beautiful stained glass windows, gold and silver crosses, silk embroideries, and wall paintings to decorate their local churches. They also paid to keep candles burning close to statues of favorite saints—especially the Virgin Mary—and for priests to say special masses for themselves, their families, and their friends. They believed that the saints and the masses could help dead souls leave purgatory—a place where the souls of Christians who had sinned during their lives were sent for punishment until they were pure enough to enter heaven.

Meeting a Need

It was almost impossible for 16th-century men and women to be atheists or agnostics. The modern, scientific, rational view of the world had not yet been invented. Heaven, hell, purgatory, and miracles worked by God and the saints seemed very real. At a time when

Human and divine meet face to face in this Flemish painting that shows wealthy donors and their children kneeling in front of Jesus, the Virgin Mary, angels, and saints.

Like many other thoughtful, educated Catholics, Dutch humanist scholar Desiderius Erasmus (c.1469–1536) called for change from within the Church. His ideas influenced many later reformers, especially Martin Luther.

life was uncertain, and often cut short by accidents, childbirth, or disease, most people needed the Church, and relied on it. In one study of northern England, historians found that over three-quarters of the men and women who made wills left goods or money to the Church.

A Sense of Failure

In other ways, the Church was not secure. Although Pope Gregory VII (reigned 1073–1085) had confidently proclaimed that:

 the Roman Church has never been wrong, nor can it be wrong until the end of time,

people saw how Church leaders, and sometimes their own parish priests, were weak or corrupt, and failed to fulfill their duties. They witnessed sordid power struggles between Church leaders and local rulers over politics, taxes, and land.

They did not know about the learned discussions of Catholic scholars, and would not have understood them. Most were frightened of knowing too much about heretics' ideas in case they themselves were accused. However, many ordinary people had overheard comments similar to those of Paul Lomely, of Gravesend in Kent, England, who complained in 1524 that:

these priests maketh us to believe that the…bread they hold…is God, and it is but a cake!

And some, especially if they lived in towns, would have come across copies of books designed to be read by questioning Christians at home—for example, *The Sum of Holy Scripture*, which said that faith was more important than penance. They might also have seen new translations of the Bible into European languages. These were described in 1527 by one English preacher as:

swords of our savior Christ

—potentially powerful weapons with which to attack the Church. Although few people at the time realized it, the long process of Reformation had begun.

The Gutenberg Bible was published around 1453–1456. It was one of the first books to be printed with movable type in Europe. Its publication, while in Latin, opened the way for printers to produce numerous Bible translations in the forthcoming decades.

PROTESTING PERSONALITIES

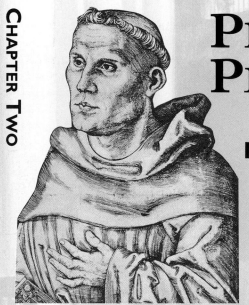

A lifelike portrait of Martin Luther, drawn by German artist Lucas Cranach the Elder in 1520.

Martin Luther

The Reformation was not caused by individual men or women. But it would not have happened so fast, or spread so widely, without the influence of several remarkable personalities. The most important of these was a German Roman Catholic monk and professor of theology named Martin Luther, who lived from 1483 to 1546.

The Gift of Grace

Like many other Catholic scholars before him, Luther liked to discuss how and why Christian souls were saved. In particular, he was interested in penance and good works. His ideas were challenging but, at first, not heretical. He believed that:

we are not made righteous (good) by doing righteous deeds, but when we have become righteous, then we do good deeds.

Luther argued that God alone made people good, through his divine gift of grace. Good works, such as giving to charity, were important as signs of goodness. But by themselves, without God's grace, they did not bring salvation.

This scathing 16th-century cartoon portrays the Pope (seated, left) selling indulgences.

Indulgences

In 1517 Luther was angered by the activities of a friar named Johann Tetzel (c.1465–1519), who was traveling through Germany, preaching and selling indulgences. These were official Church documents guaranteed to limit a dead soul's time in purgatory in return for a large fee. Luther thought that indulgences were morally corrupt—it was wicked to sell salvation—and theologically wrong. If, as he believed, God made people good though grace, then indulgences were pointless. If people had grace, their souls did not need the help of indulgences. But if they did not have grace, indulgences could not help them. Indulgences were simply a greedy trick to mislead uneducated Christian men and women and extort money from them.

Debating the Issues

In Luther's time, students were often taught by listening to, and taking part in, debates. It was common practice for professors to send lists of topics to other scholars, so they could read, study, pray, and prepare their arguments before joining in a public discussion. Late in 1517, Luther decided to share his complaints about indulgences. He made a list of 95 detailed points (which he called theses) that he wanted to discuss, and sent them to the local archbishop and to several German scholars. It was later claimed that he also pinned a copy of the list on the door of the most important local church, in the town of Wittenberg, but no-one knows if this is true. It would not have been an unusual thing to do. Some of the scholars who received Luther's theses were so impressed that they published them without Luther's consent, and his ideas on grace and indulgences began to spread through Europe.

Luther pinning his 95 theses to the door of Wittenberg church in 1517, as imagined by a 19th-century artist.

The Debate Grows

Luther's complaints embarrassed the archbishop, who had given Tetzel permission to preach, and infuriated Tetzel's fellow friars. They accused Luther of heresy, and the archbishop asked the Pope for advice. For political reasons, the Pope did not want to cause trouble in Wittenberg, so he sent a senior Church official to persuade Luther to give up his complaints quietly. But Luther refused. Instead, he wrote books and pamphlets to explain his views. Before long, many different Catholic scholars joined in the debate about indulgences on both sides.

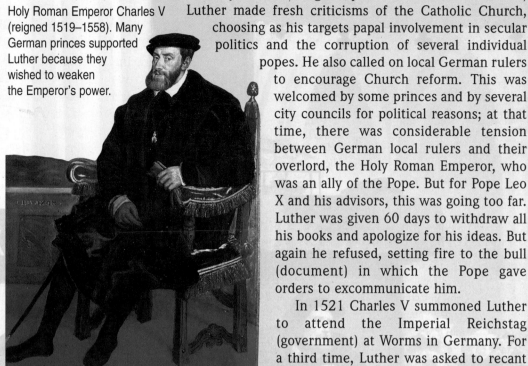

Holy Roman Emperor Charles V (reigned 1519–1558). Many German princes supported Luther because they wished to weaken the Emperor's power.

Luther preaching at Wartburg Castle in 1521 under the protection of a German prince who supported his call for Church reform. Without encouragement from local rulers in Germany, Luther's ideas might never have spread so far or so fast.

Excommunicated

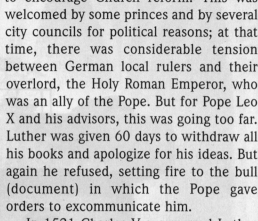

In the years following the publication of his 95 theses, Luther made fresh criticisms of the Catholic Church, choosing as his targets papal involvement in secular politics and the corruption of several individual popes. He also called on local German rulers to encourage Church reform. This was welcomed by some princes and by several city councils for political reasons; at that time, there was considerable tension between German local rulers and their overlord, the Holy Roman Emperor, who was an ally of the Pope. But for Pope Leo X and his advisors, this was going too far. Luther was given 60 days to withdraw all his books and apologize for his ideas. But again he refused, setting fire to the bull (document) in which the Pope gave orders to excommunicate him.

In 1521 Charles V summoned Luther to attend the Imperial Reichstag (government) at Worms in Germany. For a third time, Luther was asked to recant but said he could not—it would be against his conscience and against the word of God, revealed in the Bible, and so neither safe nor honest. A few weeks later, the Church condemned Luther and his followers as heretics. Their lives were now in danger. To protect Luther, a sympathetic German prince arranged to have him kidnapped and locked up in a castle. In this safe retreat, Luther continued to write, and to prepare a German translation of the Bible.

The Importance of Faith

In captivity, Luther developed and explained his ideas about salvation. He thought that faith (belief and trust in God, gained through prayer and Bible study) grew within individual men and women as they learned to know God and love him. He argued that Christians with faith, helped by God's grace, had no need for priests, good works, or the sacraments of the Church. Instead, their souls were saved through a spiritual process of cleansing and rebirth, which Luther called justification.

If Christian souls were saved by grace and faith, and not by the sacraments, then the Church was not only useless as a means of salvation, but might also hinder many people seeking to know and trust God. Its magical (or miraculous) rituals seemed like simple, vulgar superstition rather than holy mysteries.

The Peasants' War

Luther's ideas had a revolutionary impact on the minds of many priests and scholars who were already calling for Church reform, and also on less educated or less judicious people. These included radical preachers who inflamed feelings and raised expectations among peasant farmers taking part in a mass rebellion in southern Germany. This "Peasants' War" (1524–1526) was caused by poor harvests and rural poverty. But in the heated atmosphere following Luther's protests, wild, revolutionary religious ideas began to circulate among the rebels. They hoped that Jesus would soon return to Earth, bringing social equality and justice. Luther, however, was horrified by their violence, and supported the local rulers' fight against them. By the time the war was over, around 100,000 peasant rebels had been killed.

This sensitive drawing of praying hands, made by German artist Albrecht Durer in 1508, has since been used to symbolize individual communication with God.

A New Church

In 1525 Luther married a former nun. Like many Church critics, he believed that compulsory celibacy for priests was wrong. He spent the later years of his life at home preaching, teaching, and writing. But his influence continued to grow. His followers, led by Philip Melanchthon, broke away from the Catholic Church to set up a new Church of their own, which spread through Germany, Scandinavia, and the Netherlands. It became known as Lutheran, and still has many members. Printed copies of Luther's books and sermons were sent to questioning Christians all over Europe, who welcomed his ideas and accepted his new views on grace and faith. His translation of the Bible was acclaimed as a great work of literature, and is still admired today.

21

Zwingli's influence in Zurich led to the abolition of religious images, the introduction of a reformist liturgy, and the closure of monasteries.

The Circles Widen

Germany was probably the most important early center of the debate on the need for Church reform, but reforming thinkers and scholars were active throughout Europe, from Iceland to states that bordered the Muslim Ottoman empire. In Switzerland, Germany's neighbor, rival cities and cantons (states) with opposing religious views fought a bitter war from 1529–1531. One of the most famous casualties was reformer Huldrych Zwingli (1484–1531). He was strongly influenced by Erasmus, but departed further from the traditional teachings of the Catholic Church, especially regarding the key doctrine of transubstantiation (see page 15). He spearheaded the movement for reform in his home city of Zurich, and was killed fighting alongside fellow citizens to defend their beliefs and independence. But by that time, his ideas had spread to England, where they had a powerful influence among reformers like Thomas Cranmer (see page 28).

Jean Calvin

A second Swiss reformer, Jean Calvin (1509–1564), was even more influential. One historian has described him as giving the reform movement a "second wind." Born in France a generation later than Luther, Calvin settled in Geneva around 1538, and from 1541 to 1564 dominated the reformed Church and city government there. From 1550 on, his ideas on doctrine and Church organization spread to many parts of Europe, where they shaped the reformed Churches of France, the Netherlands,

A view of the Swiss city of Geneva, where Calvin and his supporters aimed to create a reformed, Christian government.

Scotland, and to a lesser extent, England. His masterwork, *Christianae Religionis Institutio* (generally known as the *Institutes*), first published in 1536, laid down guidelines for all reformed Churches. Calvin's city, Geneva, became famous as a place where political and religious reform proceeded step by step together, and where Church laws shaped state policy. Calvin's aim in was to create a "godly commonwealth" where reformed Christians could live safely.

Predestination

Calvin's religious writings and the example of his reformed commonwealth in Geneva were highly influential, particularly in Switzerland, England, Scotland, and later, North America.

Like all other reformers, Calvin opposed many traditional and popular Catholic practices, such as confession and penance, prayers to saints, veneration of relics, going on pilgrimages, and the sale of indulgences. But his most influential teaching related to the key issue of salvation. He believed in predestination, declaring that God alone chose people to be saved. Predestination was not a totally new idea. Earlier Catholic scholars had discussed it, usually as part of their consideration of the eternal question faced by religious people of all faiths— why does God allow sin and suffering in the world?

The Catholic answer was that God gave people free will, which allowed them to sin, and thereby lose salvation if they chose. But Calvin provided an alternative answer. God had chosen to save some people, but not others. How else could sin and suffering be explained, except by supposing that they were inherently "programmed" by God? In his *Institutes*, Calvin says:

We call predestination God's eternal decree, by which he compacted [agreed] with himself what he willed to become for each man. For all are not created in equal condition; rather, eternal life is foreordained for some, eternal damnation for others.

Logically, the doctrine of predestination complemented and completed Luther's belief in justification by faith. All reformers agreed that the faith and grace required for salvation were gifts from God; Calvin taught that predestination was a gift also. No man or woman could ever hope to earn it, nor could people know whether they were predestined to be saved, but the thought of it was, according to English Protestant writers in 1563:

full of sweet, pleasant and unspeakable comfort to godly persons.

23

A Growing Movement

By 1550, what had started as a series of isolated, individual, or small-group protests against laziness and corruption in the Church had turned into a widespread reforming movement. It involved unconventional religious radicals as well as deeply respected Church scholars, and a range of very different opinions. Besides Lollards, Hussites, and Lutherans, there were Zwinglians and Calvinists, Mennonites, and other Anabaptists (see page 43).

Scholarly debates, printing, and the Renaissance-inspired fashion for philosophical letters spread the reformers' ideas among the educated. Public preaching, political gossip, and simple cartoon-style woodcuts extended these ideas to ordinary men and women.

Powerful Support

The initial success of calls for reform depended on several factors. The personality and political ability of the reformer, or group of reformers, was obviously very important. The state of the local church, the quality of the local clergy, and the attitude of local political elites also had a key part to play in promoting or stifling reform. Often, religious and political issues were closely linked. In Scandinavia, for example, where the Swedish and Danish kings were sympathetic to Church reform and opposed to politically ambitious local Catholic bishops, the reformed, Lutheran Church became the state-sanctioned form of Christianity soon after 1550. In contrast, Germany remained deeply troubled by religious quarrels for over 100 years. In Luther's time, German land was divided into over 100 small states, under the overlordship of the Catholic Holy Roman Emperor. But each state had its own local ruler, and the majority in the north, center, and southeast supported reform. Their views were shared by several rich and powerful free cities. In 1530 the princes joined together in the Schmalkaldic League—an alliance against the Catholic Emperor. They were not powerful enough to achieve their demands, but their action still threatened to destabilize the European balance of political power.

Differences

The reformers did not all share the same beliefs, or have the same hopes for change. For example, Luther believed

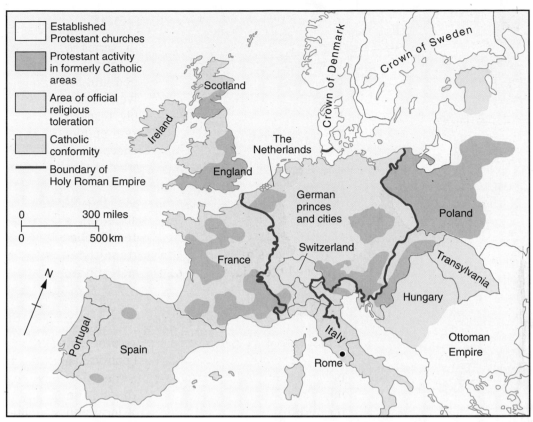

A map showing the spread of Protestantism in the early 16th century.

Since many people could not read, public preaching was especially important in spreading the reformers' message.

that moderate-paced reform of Church organization should be preceded by public education and understanding, while Zwingli (and Calvin) took the opposite view. Zwingli, in particular, argued that changes in Church structure and ways of worshiping should be made as quickly as possible, since they were the outward reflection of vital new inner truths. The reformers were, however, united in one main objection to traditional Catholic Church teaching—that confession and acts of penance could wipe away sin. Only God could do that, either through his gifts of grace and faith, or by predestination.

In spite of their differences, most reformers were labeled as Protestants by their opponents. The term is still used to describe members of non-Catholic Churches today. It originated in 1529 when a group of German princes staged a formal protest at a meeting of the Imperial Parliament in Speyer, Germany, to oppose a resolution, strongly backed by the Holy Roman Emperor, that Church reform should

RELIGION AND POLITICS

Mixed Motives

In the early 16th century, kings and princes knew they could not introduce new religious ideas without the support of influential groups in society. Few dared risk straining alliances or provoking wars solely on account of them. Why, then, did many rulers support religious change? Almost always, it promised the welcome prospect of financial gain by taking over Church property and lands, and the resulting opportunity to recruit more political support. But it also raised the terrifying possibility of civil unrest or rebellion. It meant freedom from irksome interference in national affairs from the international Catholic Church, but resulted in new responsibilities for overseeing Church law, discipline, and administration. Religion and politics were inseparable, especially so in England, where religious beliefs and political issues became entangled with the emotional and dynastic needs of King Henry VIII (reigned 1509–1547).

Defender of the Faith?

Henry VIII's own beliefs were Catholic. In 1521 the Pope awarded him the title "Defender of the Faith" for supporting Catholic sacraments against Luther's views. Backed by his chief minister, Cardinal Thomas Wolsey, Henry also persecuted reforming priests and scholars and forced many Protestant sympathizers into exile. Of the few reformers who remained, almost all were tried for heresy and executed.

Initially, Henry's politics were Catholic as well. In 1509 he married Catherine of Aragon, aunt of Catholic Charles V—the Holy Roman Emperor and a powerful ally of England. But Catherine failed to give birth to a son and heir. By the late 1520s, Henry calculated that it would be in England's strategic interests to weaken his alliance with Charles.

At the same time, he quarreled with the Pope over what became known as "the King's Great Matter"— his demand for a divorce. Henry wanted a new wife to

Henry VIII of England saw himself as a Catholic reformer of the Church.

provide a male heir, and desired Anne Boleyn, a young noblewoman whose support of Church reform further complicated the situation. However, in 1527, the papal city Rome was occupied by Charles V's troops. Charles V would not see his aunt dishonored and forced the Pope to refuse Henry a divorce. But Henry would not give up. In 1529 he began to harass senior Church officials, including Wolsey. When this proved fruitless, Henry decided that to get a divorce he would have to change the organization of the English Church.

Cardinal Thomas Wolsey (1474–1530), Henry VIII's chief minister, fell from royal favor after failing to negotiate Henry's divorce.

Royal Supremacy

In 1531 Henry bullied the Catholic bishops into declaring him:

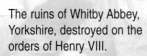 *sole protector and supreme head of the English Church and clergy, so far as the law of God allows.*

In 1533 his ministers persuaded Parliament to pass laws stating that religious cases, including divorce, could only be decided by Church courts in England. The same year, using these new laws, Henry divorced Catherine and married Anne, who was by now pregnant. (She disappointingly gave birth to a daughter, Elizabeth.) In 1534 Parliament passed the Act of Supremacy, confirming that:

The King's majesty justly and rightfully is and ought to be the supreme head of the Church in England.

The ruins of Whitby Abbey, Yorkshire, destroyed on the orders of Henry VIII.

It also outlawed payment of taxes to the Pope. Priests and heads of religious houses were forced, on pain of death, to swear an oath of loyalty to the King.

In 1535 Henry commissioned Thomas Cromwell to arrange inspections of monasteries and nunneries. Ostensibly, this was to check for signs of religious shortcomings, but it also punished the monastic heads who had refused to accept Henry as head of the Church. Cromwell also compiled the *Valor Ecclesiaticus*, a survey of monastic wealth. This was an ominous sign. On Henry's orders, between 1536 and 1540, all 800 English monasteries were closed, in spite of considerable local opposition, and their property was sold. Henry's government got the profits.

Scholar, diplomat, and, later, Archbishop of Canterbury, Thomas Cranmer (1489–1556) gradually became a supporter of Lutheran reforms.

The accession of Edward VI (reigned 1547–1553) to the English throne proved a turning point in the English Church.

Still Catholic

To obtain his divorce, Henry VIII had changed the way the Church was run, but he had not interfered in matters of belief. Doctrinally, the Church in England was still Catholic. But beginning in the mid-1530s, a group of Protestant sympathizers at the royal court, led by Thomas Cranmer (from 1533, Archbishop of Canterbury) and Thomas Cromwell, tried to introduce Protestant reforms. Henry, however, would not agree. They did persuade him, though, to allow the first official translation of the Bible into English in 1537.

After the execution of Anne Boleyn in 1536 and the death of Henry's third wife, Jane Seymour, while giving birth to his only son in 1537, Henry needed another wife. In 1540 Cromwell suggested Anne, daughter of the reform-minded Prince of Cleves. He anticipated that this marriage alliance would provide political and theological support for Church reforms. But soon after the wedding, Henry rejected Anne, and with her, closer links to the German princes. Cromwell was executed on Henry's orders. From then until Henry's death in 1547, religious policies were unsettled, depending on short-term political pressures or the King's whim. One historian wrote:

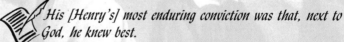

His [Henry's] most enduring conviction was that, next to God, he knew best.

This allowed for no substantial doctrinal reform.

A Careful Balance

Henry VIII was a shrewd, intelligent, and experienced politician. But even he found it difficult to reconcile the conflicting demands of Catholic priests, Protestant ministers, politicians, military advisors, reforming scholars, ordinary people, and his own conscience. He managed to maintain his own preferred, basically Catholic, faith by what one historian has called a "cruelly careful balance" between reformers and traditionalists, playing off one faction against another, often bloodily. In 1547 Henry's only son, 9-year-old Edward VI, became the new king. Obviously, he could not manage Church and state, religion and politics, as his father had done.

England Becomes Protestant

Edward VI's reign saw major changes in the teachings of the Church in England, which became decisively Protestant for the first time. This did not displease young Edward, who was being educated by reform-minded tutors. But he did not control the process as his father had done. Instead, powerful people in England who sympathized with Protestant reforms saw their chance to implement doctrinal change now that Henry VIII was dead.

In his will, Henry VIII named a 16-man Council of Regents to govern the country for Edward. But before it was able to take charge of Edward's government, Edward Seymour, who became Duke of Somerset, seized power. Somerset supported Protestantism for political reasons. In 1548 he allowed Cranmer to introduce cautious changes to the Church in England. In 1549 the first Prayer Book in English was introduced, arguably the most revolutionary change ever made to worship in England. The laws against heretics were repealed.

The 1549 Prayer Book marked a revolutionary change in worship, replacing the familiar Latin mass with new rituals in English.

SPECIMENS OF THE FIRST BOOK OF COMMON PRAYER.

In the same year, however, Somerset was removed from power in a *coup d'état* led by military commander John Dudley, later Duke of Northumberland. Northumberland won the confidence of teenage Edward VI, and let Cranmer press ahead with more sweeping changes to the Church. These included a new, more Calvinist Prayer Book in 1552, and a basically Protestant statement of beliefs, the 42 Articles, in 1553. Cranmer also encouraged reformers who had left England under Henry VIII to return, along with Protestant scholars and preachers from Switzerland and Germany. But his plans for further reform came to an abrupt halt in 1553, when young King Edward died.

A Mixed Reaction

The Edwardian reforms were introduced piecemeal, always with one eye to the government's wider political aims at home and overseas. Moreover, Protestantism did not lead to peace. In 1549 riots broke out in 23 English counties. They were partly caused by poor harvests and growing poverty, but religious changes, especially the new Prayer Book, also played a part. Many rebels were hostile to new doctrines, declaring that:

 they would keep the old and ancient religion as their forefathers had done.

Elsewhere, quarrels between priests and the people over revised Church taxes contributed to many local disputes.

Who Should Be Queen?

After Edward's death in 1553, Northumberland tried to have his Protestant daughter-in-law, Lady Jane Grey, recognized as queen. By birth, Henry's VIII's daughters, Mary and Elizabeth, had better rights to rule than Lady Jane. But Henry had once declared both of them illegitimate (though he later changed his mind) and, compared to Lady Jane, they had few powerful noble supporters. Even so, Mary was determined to claim the throne. To Northumberland's surprise, many thousands of ordinary people marched toward London to support her. She was proclaimed queen, and people in many parts of England:

greatly rejoiced, making great fires, drinking wine and ale, and praising God.

Mary, a devout Catholic, planned to reverse the changes that had been made to the Church in England during Henry and Edward's reigns. Legally, this was not simple or straightforward. Cromwell, Somerset, and Northumberland had taken care to involve Parliament in making all the organizational changes to the Church, and many of its members supported the movement for Church reform. The issue of royal supremacy was especially awkward. Few politicians, even if they were Catholic, were willing to hand back legal, financial, and administrative rights to the papacy—a foreign power.

But by 1554, after much political maneuvring and considerable pressure, the Catholic Church was restored in England, legally and doctrinally. It proved impossible, however, to persuade most people who had legally

Mary I (reigned 1553–1558) was welcomed by many people who disliked the religious reforms of Edward VI's reign.

purchased Church property to give up their new possessions. Some priests and parishioners, however, did manage to recover church furnishings, crosses, and gold and silver, and were encouraged to replace them if the old ones could not be found. Mary's actions matched the mood of uncertainty among many ordinary people. They disliked repeated religious turmoil and uncertainty, and were not yet familiar with Protestant services. As one of Edward VI's advisors had commented:

the use of the new [religion] is not yet printed in the stomachs of eleven of twelve parts of the realm.

This 16th-century image shows the French capture of Calais in 1558—a desperate humiliation for the English.

"Bloody Mary"

However, in 1554 Mary took a step that alarmed most English people. She married Philip, son and heir of Catholic Emperor Charles V. England had never been ruled by a queen, much less one who was married, and many English people predicted that their nation's political independence would be compromised. These fears seemed justified when in 1558 England, fighting as an ally of Spain, lost its only continental territory, the port of Calais, in a disastrous war against France.

Mary also revived the old heresy laws, which condemned obdurate heretics to a horrific death. She may not have set out to be brutal—she sent instructions that prosecutions should "not [be] done by rashness"—but she probably did hope to intimidate. Over 280 men and women were burned alive for refusing to give up their Protestant beliefs. After Mary's death these executions were used to generate maximum publicity for the Protestant cause.

After Mary's death, supporters of reform issued anti-Catholic propaganda, like this image of a heretic's execution, published in 1563 in John Foxe's *Acts and Monuments*, popularly known as *Foxe's Book of Martyrs*.

Opposing Forces

The experience of each European country during the years of reform was unique. But England serves to highlight, in a rather extreme form, many of the difficulties, or opportunities, faced by 16th-century reformers, and also the issues confronting rulers trying to manage religious change. Monarchs and princes often had to perform a balancing act to reconcile the opposing forces of religious fervor and political control. This was of crucial importance at a time when many people considered the spiritual and supernatural as the absolute foundation of their lives and the decider of their souls' eternal destiny.

Years of Upheaval

By the time of Mary's death in 1558, England had lived through almost 30 years of religious upheaval affecting three successive generations. A sizable proportion of the population—even stalwarts on both sides of the religious divide—felt confused and unsettled by this rapid change.

Religious change touched not only peoples' beliefs and ways of worship, but also their material surroundings (churches were usually the largest buildings in any community) and the way they thought about their everyday lives. The bloodshed in the name of religion, from the judicial murders sanctioned by Henry VIII to the persecutions of Mary I's reign, had been traumatic.

Europe Divided

Religious tensions combined with political differences to create a heightened emotional climate. By the mid-16th century, there had been wars and rebellions with a religious dimension in England, Germany, Switzerland, and several other European states. Religious differences could serve as a useful lever for dissidents at home (the 16th century was a time of economic crises and rapid social change) as well as for enemy states overseas, hungry for power and land. By the end of Mary I's reign (1558), the states of Europe were painfully divided (see map on page 33). For almost the next 100 years, religion also played a key part in international relations, often with tragic consequences.

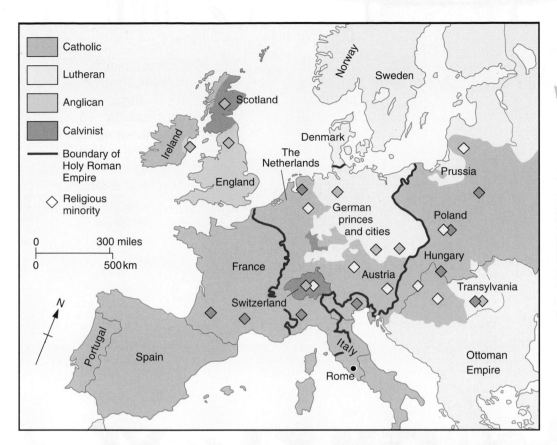

A map showing Protestant and Catholic power blocs during the reigns of Elizabeth I of England and Philip II of Spain, c.1560.

Map legend:
- Catholic
- Lutheran
- Anglican
- Calvinist
- Boundary of Holy Roman Empire
- Religious minority

0   300 miles
0   500 km

N

Map labels: Norway, Sweden, Scotland, Ireland, Denmark, The Netherlands, Prussia, England, German princes and cities, Poland, France, Hungary, Austria, Transylvania, Switzerland, Portugal, Spain, Italy, Rome, Ottoman Empire

The Elizabethan Settlement

This unenviable situation faced Mary's sister, Elizabeth I, when she became queen. In religion, she seems to have held moderately Protestant beliefs, although some Catholic traditions of worship, especially church music, appealed to her aesthetic sense. Like almost all other European rulers, Elizabeth faced two major problems—stability at home and security from foreign invasion.

Elizabeth's first priority was to negotiate a political and religious compromise to end England's religious upheavals. This Elizabethan Settlement combined Henry VIII's royal supremacy and reorganization of the Church in England with the doctrinal changes introduced during Edward VI's reign. No other religious traditions were approved or tolerated. The Settlement was traditional enough to appeal to conservative-minded clergy and lay people, while former Church critics could claim that it was reformed.

Raised in surroundings of personal danger and political intrigue, Elizabeth I was an immensely skillful politician. Her religious settlement was a shrewd combination of many old, well-loved rituals and moderate doctrinal changes.

PART II: REFORMED RELIGION

NEW WAYS TO WORSHIP

Ignorance or Understanding?

It is difficult to know exactly how much of the reformers' complicated theological arguments ordinary people understood. Luther himself complained:

 The common man, especially in the villages, knows absolutely nothing about Christian doctrine.

Few peasants had any understanding of the finer points of Catholic religious teaching. But through their attendance at church, most medieval villagers were familiar with basic Christian concepts, and many had strong views about priests' behavior and the Church's institutional corruption.

People who lived in towns were often better educated (some were literate) and politically sophisticated. Ideas spread more quickly in towns, where people lived close together and had the opportunity to hear and debate new views. As a result, townspeople with an interest in the reformers' message probably could understand its main points, at least in simple form. For instance, in 1525 a group of citizens in Strasbourg, France, called for the abolition of masses to save souls because:

Christ has done everything for all believers.

This was one of Luther's key teachings, which they had clearly grasped.

For others—probably the large majority of ordinary people—understanding and, more importantly, accepting religious change was more difficult. If people did not understand why change was necessary, reformed ways of worship and the removal of many Catholic church traditions looked like vandalism. They therefore resisted innovation. For example, Swiss-born reformer Martin Bucer (1482–1531) commented that, in England, religious changes were:

Reformer John Knox (c.1513–72) led the reorganization of the Kirk (Church) in Scotland on Calvinist lines. As this dramatic 19th-century painting suggests, he was famous for his forceful preaching.

for the most part carried on by the means of ordinances [laws], which the majority obey very grudgingly.

A New Ritual

New laws introduced profound changes to patterns of Christian worship. In all Protestant countries, the Catholic Church's most important ritual, the mass, was abolished and replaced by a new, simpler service. This was known by various names, such as Holy Communion or the Lord's Supper. It became a ceremony commemorating Jesus' last meal with his disciples and his death on the cross, rather than a magical reenactment of his sacrifice.

Reformers were bitterly divided on how Jesus was present at the new service, but they all agreed that there was no transubstantiation of the bread and wine into his body, as the Catholic Church taught. Luther was the most conservative, arguing that while real bread and real wine existed throughout the service, it was possible and permissible for worshipers to believe that Jesus' body existed in them also. Zwingli was the most extreme in rejecting transubstantiation, declaring that:

the bread and wine...are...the symbolic body of Christ.

Calvin's views were open to different interpretations. He argued that Jesus' body was not physically present at the service, but that his flesh and blood nevertheless fed the soul.

Consolidation

The reformers also agreed on another major change—that preaching to explain and consolidate reformed doctrine should play a much larger part in worship. In this they were supported by many Protestant rulers, especially those who wanted to ensure religious uniformity within their lands. Most rulers prudently imposed systems, such as oaths or licences, to make sure that preachers' doctrine was of a kind they approved.

A preacher—Bible in hand—explains his reforming ideas to a Lutheran congregation in Denmark in 1561, while Holy Communion is administered.

Why Have Sacraments?

Besides replacing the mass, reformers also radically altered the other Catholic sacraments. Only two—communion and baptism—originated from Jesus' own practice as recorded in the Bible. The rest had developed during the early years of the Catholic Church. Reformers asked whether sacraments were necessary if God saved people through his gifts of grace and faith. Most decided that they were, although not all seven previously practiced by the Catholic Church. To reformers, sacraments were outward signs of an inner, spiritual state. They existed, in Luther's words, "to nourish faith"—that is, to encourage Christian believers and strengthen their hopes of salvation.

Communion, which replaced the mass (see page 15), was the most important Protestant sacrament. Baptism was also vital. The Catholic Church taught that it washed away the original sin that each baby was born with, but reformers argued that it had a deeper significance. It was a way of completely cleansing and fortifying the soul so that, as Calvin explained:

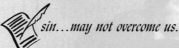

sin…may not overcome us.

However, the reformers considered the other five Catholic sacraments, including confession and penance, to be mere rituals of the Church, and they abolished or downgraded them.

New Professionals

These theological decisions affected more than abstract belief—they shaped Church organization. If sacraments were less important in reformed Churches, what were reformed priests (known as pastors or ministers) needed for? Could services, or even sacraments, take place without them? Most reformers believed that ministers were needed, but that their duties should be very different from those of Catholic priests. Their tasks were to preach, teach, and encourage ordinary people to lead godly lives.

At first, many reformed clergy were existing Catholic parish priests who accepted, willingly or unwillingly, the religious changes imposed on them by rulers or leading members of their local community. But as they died or retired, a new generation of Protestant ministers grew up. They were enthusiasts who had chosen the reformed faith and were deeply committed to it. Unlike

Catholic priests, who believed that their whole nature had been transformed by ordination, Protestant ministers saw themselves as trained religious professionals with a job to do. They were well-educated, especially in theology, and were mostly recruited from a narrow social range (the upper and middle ranks of urban society). Unlike Catholic priests, almost all were married, and some founded dynasties of reformers as their sons and grandsons trained for the ministry to replace them.

New Organizations

The reformed view of a minister's duties also helped determine the leadership structure, decision-making processes, and administrative "machinery" of each new reformed Church. Congregations were now expected to play a larger part. New Protestant churches were organized in many different ways—in great contrast to the uniform structure of the international Catholic Church. Some reformed Churches, like the Church in England, were Episcopal—they were led by bishops and archbishops who supervised ministers and congregations in a greatly simplified version of traditional Catholic Church structure. Others, like Calvin's Church in Geneva, or the Church of Scotland, were Presbyterian. Each Presbyterian congregation was led by a minister assisted by elders (respected members of the congregation). The whole Church organization was governed by assemblies of representatives, elected from ministers and elders by members of several congregations.

Calvinists meeting for worship in Lyons, France, in 1565. The pulpit (stand for the preacher) is the focal point of the building.

Plain and Simple

Reformers taught that salvation was now a matter of spiritual hope and trust rather than a bargain with God achieved through penance and good works. By implication, this meant that all other materialistic superstitions, such as charms or holy relics, were also worthless. As they studied and discussed the importance of salvation by faith, and the worthlessness of many sacraments, some reformers began to question whether formal worship was necessary at all. They decided that it was, but that it ought to be much plainer and simpler than the elaborate, sometimes theatrical, rituals of the traditional Catholic Church. They set out to purify ways of worshiping by removing everything that was not directly related to the two surviving Protestant sacraments.

This "stripping of the altars" happened in different ways in different countries. In England, for example, in the 1540s Edward VI's government gave orders to priests and parishioners to remove all images of saints, elaborate crosses, and silver cups and plates used in mass from their churches. The elaborate silk robes, decorated with gold or jewels, worn by priests and bishops for church services were also to be taken away. Wall paintings and stained glass windows showing Catholic subjects, such as saints and their miracles, were covered with whitewash or destroyed. In 1550 parishes were instructed to dismantle their altars—richly decorated platforms (almost resembling theater stages) where the dramatic ritual of mass was performed—and to replace them with plain wooden tables suitable for celebrating the Lord's Supper.

Superstitious Symbols?

These religious furnishings were often works of art. Ordinary people were attached to them, partly for their beauty, partly because they told lively stories (stained glass windows were nicknamed "the poor man's Bible"), and partly because they were linked to their everyday lives. If parishioners were wealthy, they or their ancestors might have paid for a painting or a statue to decorate a church as a family memorial. If they were less rich, they might have contributed to a collection or taken part in community fundraising to buy something beautiful for their local church.

Destroying these objects was, in effect, destroying or devaluing their own past. But to the reformers, and reform-minded believers, these elaborate church furnishings were examples of superstition and wrong belief. Like the discredited sacrament of penance and the sale of indulgences, pictures, statues, and other rich furnishings suggested that salvation might be purchased by generous gifts to the Church. They also encouraged idolatry—for example, ignorant people worshiped religious objects as if they were holy themselves, rather than understanding that they were just symbols of religious truths or reminders of saints' holy lives. Like church music, processions, candles, and incense, they took people's minds away from the plain simple truth revealed in the Bible. All these:

sundry superstitious things, tending to the maintenance of idolatry

had to go. The only music allowed in many plainly decorated Protestant Churches were simple chants and psalms.

These two 17th-century churches illustrate changing styles in church decoration. The plain, simple interior of the reformed church (left) contrasts greatly with the grand, elaborate architecture and rich decoration of the Catholic church.

How Welcome?

It is impossible to generalize about how welcome these changes to worship were. In some places, particularly towns, citizens—or influential groups of them—welcomed the reformers' ideas. They eagerly joined in the destruction of superstitious church furnishings, and devoutly attended new-style purified services. In other places, parishioners fought with workmen (there were even fatalities) to defend their treasured church ornaments. In some places, crosses, statues, and other church ornaments were carefully taken down and hidden in the hope that the wheel of change might turn full circle, and they would be approved for use once again. In these conservative places—mostly villages—parishioners only reluctantly attended new, reformed Churches, and a few refused to take part in reformed communion services at all, demanding instead the old-style mass.

Almost everywhere, on one level, it proved very difficult to make a clean break with the Catholic past. Over the centuries, religious ceremonies and popular social customs had become closely intertwined. Even in areas that welcomed reform, several ancient Catholic festivals and celebrations still survived in disguised or secularized forms—for example, Halloween. This was originally All Hallows' Eve, the night before All Saints

A Protestant mob destroys church art treasures and holy relics during a religious riot in France, 1566.

Day, when Catholic prayers were said (or paid for) to help free all Christian souls from purgatory and speed them toward heaven—a doctrine the reformers decidedly were against.

Continuing Differences

Differences of opinion existed even in countries where the religious views of the nation were decided by the state, which didn't allow dissent. In England, where laws in Elizabeth I's reign made regular attendance at church compulsory and refusal to take communion a serious offense, people opposed to reform kept their views to themselves and sullenly or reluctantly conformed. But wealthy, powerful people could afford to have their religious cake and eat it. At least two noble families in England during Elizabeth's reign kept Protestant chaplains, and Catholic priests as "tutors"—one to show conformity, and one so they could worship secretly in the way they preferred—though this was strictly against the law.

Shaped by the Past

A female priest leads worshipers at the Lord's Supper in a Protestant church, in 1994. The ordination of women is a deeply controversial issue.
It is opposed by the Catholic Church, and also by some Protestants.

Even today, styles of worship in Catholic and Protestant Churches are not just a matter of taste. They have profound meaning in religious and social terms. They symbolize a different understanding of the role of the Christian Church and its officials. In the same way, the appearance of today's church buildings is also deeply symbolic. Catholic churches tend to be richly decorated, encouraging the use of visual and audible signals to show that the space itself is holy, and to lead people's minds toward God. Lay people are often kept away from the sanctuary (the holy area around the altar, where mass is said) by screens or steps. Protestant buildings tend to be much plainer, and are furnished with pulpits or similar furniture that emphasize the key role of preaching in reformed worship. A copy of the Bible is usually prominently displayed, and the altar is positioned to reflect the communal nature of worship, especially the Lord's Supper. The organizational structures of today's Church are also not a matter of chance, but sprang from deep convictions about the differing roles of priests and people. Until very recently, Catholic priests and Protestant ministers were often reluctant to worship publicly together, even though they were all men (and occasionally women) of God.

GODLY PEOPLE?

CHAPTER FIVE

John Bunyan's *Pilgrim's Progress* (1678) is one of the world's best-loved Protestant stories. It describes the obstacles encountered by those who desire to live a godly life, and the perseverance needed to overcome them.

Priests or People?

One of the reformers' most radical ideas was that a priest was not always necessary to mediate religious experience. They believed that an individual could, through God's grace, understand divine truth by himself or herself, and communicate directly with God in prayer. Even more startling was the closely linked belief in the priesthood of all believers. The Catholic Church taught that priests were a special kind of person (always male), who had been set apart by a sacrament (ordination) that made them holy. To the reformers, this teaching profoundly contradicted their belief in God's grace and predestination. These divine gifts made people holy, not sacraments and ceremonies invented by the Church. As Luther explained:

 we are all consecrated priests through baptism.

Worship, Prayer, and Study

What did this mean in practical terms? Luther was stating what he believed to be a spiritual truth—that all baptized Christians had equal responsibilities to play an active part in the religious life of their family and wider community. This involved taking part in meetings for worship, praying publicly and in private, studying the Bible, and setting an example of good behavior. All Christians should aim to live a godly life and resist unholy temptations. But Luther, like many other leading reformers, did not expect all Christian believers to act as full-time ministers or pastors. That was a duty entrusted to a few dedicated, well-educated men, approved by their local congregations, who felt called by God to devote their lives to preaching God's word and offering consolation, counseling, admonishment, and good advice to members of their congregations. This pastoral care was necessary to help reformed Christians lead good lives. Reformers warned that a holy lifestyle would not guarantee salvation, but it was still very important because it was God's command.

A Spiritual Elite?

A few Protestant groups took this idea much further, believing that the only way for truly godly people to live was to separate themselves from the (sinful) rest of the world. Known as Anabaptists (re-baptizers) from their practice of re-baptizing all adults who wanted to join their congregations, they were regarded as dangerous extremists by rulers and many leading reformers. There were several different groups, based mostly in Germany, Switzerland, and Eastern Europe, and the precise details of their teaching varied. But they all believed that adult baptism set them apart from everyone else, including other reformed Christians. To different Anabaptist groups, baptism had different meanings. It could either be divinely inspired recognition that members were predestined to be saved, or a spiritual turning point that removed all their sins forever and compelled them thereafter to lead godly lives.

Anabaptists were among a number of groups, or sects, who were regarded as dangerous heretics by most reformers.

To achieve this godliness, Anabaptists founded separate communities where they could live in brotherly love with other members of their self-selected spiritual elite and wait for Jesus' return, as the very first Christians had done. Anyone insufficiently godly was expelled. Anabaptists refused to accept secular duties, such as military service, judicial office, or swearing oaths, and challenged many state-made laws. Sometimes this civil disobedience was passive—groups of Hutterites, for example, sought out quiet, remote places in Moravia to set up communities ruled by their own religious regulations. Sometimes it led to violence. In 1534 German Anabaptists set up a "godly kingdom" in Munster, Germany, led by a deluded (or depraved) "king of righteousness" named Jan Beukelz, who imposed many eccentric laws, including compulsory polygamy. The "kingdom" was destroyed in 1535 by an army of outraged citizens who had fled from Munster, led by their Catholic prince-bishop.

Bible Study

For Protestants, the Bible was the most important spiritual guide. It was the Holy Scripture, the Word of God, the divine truth revealed to humankind. It was far more important than any earthly institution (such as the Catholic Church) or the religious opinions of any pope, priest, or scholar, however devout and sincere. In his writings Luther frequently contrasted the authority of God's truth in the Bible with the man-made authority of the Catholic Church, and had no doubt that the Bible was more important. He was also certain that the Bible could not—and should not—be criticized by anyone:

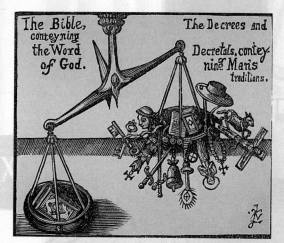

This English religious cartoon of 1676 claims that the Bible outweighs all the laws and decrees of the Pope.

The Pope, Luther...or even an angel from heaven—these should not be...judges...but only witnesses, disciples, and confessors [true believers] of Scripture.

Understanding...

The title page from an English Bible of 1539.

Finding God's message in the Bible was not always straightforward. There were problems of language and accuracy. All the reformers insisted that the Bible should be available in languages that 16th-century men and women could understand. Many also wanted to go back, if they could, to the earlier, pre-Latin manuscript versions of the Biblical text to produce a more accurate translation than the Catholic Vulgate (approved Latin version) had been.

In spite of these difficulties, by around 1600 a modern-language version of the Bible was available to almost anyone in Western Europe who could read—unless they lived in a country with a staunchly Catholic government, where reformed religious texts were banned. In some Protestant countries like England, reformed, modern-language translations were made compulsory for use in churches and private homes, to force worshipers to make a break with Catholic tradition and, reforming ministers hoped, to increase ordinary people's knowledge and awareness of the Bible's message.

...And Interpretation

To many Protestants, the chance to read and study the Bible for themselves was liberating and exciting. At last, they could "hear" the Word of God directly. But it was also unsettling and potentially dangerous to the good order and correct doctrines of the reformed Church. The Bible was not easy to interpret, even for scholars, ministers, and other experts with many years' training. Indeed, most reformers argued that it could not be understood by human reason alone. God's Holy Spirit was necessary to inspire and guide the reader. As Zwingli explained:

> *When the Word of God shines on human understanding, it enlightens it in such as way that it understands... and knows the certainty of it.*

Reformers warned ordinary Christians always to be guided by their ministers, who expounded passages from the Bible in sermons or explained them in pamphlets and broadsheets. They told educated Bible readers to bear in mind past Catholic scholarship, which could sometimes be helpful, and to constantly consider how Bible texts might help illuminate key Protestant teachings on grace and salvation. Only then, they argued, would the real truth be revealed.

A Continuing Influence

Ever since the 16th century, the Bible has played an essential part in the lives of millions of Protestant men and women, and in the worship and missionary activities of all the reformed Churches. For example, even today, more than 400 years after the reformers first preached, a large region of the United States with a Protestant majority population in the South is known as the Bible Belt. Although different groups of Protestants place a slightly different emphasis on Biblical importance, they all agree about its central role in Christian life and faith.

Reformers encouraged the study of the Bible at home, as seen in this painting (c.1675) entitled "The Bible Lesson." Some historians have suggested that this helped liberate women by allowing them equal access to the Word of God, but many women could not read. Reformers also taught that women should be silent in church, unlike men, who could preach and lead public prayers.

Free to Disagree?

Radical, breakaway Protestant movements like the Anabaptists, and free access to powerful texts like the Bible, showed how some reformers' theological teachings were potentially subversive, or even revolutionary. Although reformed Church leaders were reluctant to acknowledge it, direct access to God through prayer and the inspired reading of his Word, in effect, constituted a kind of freedom of conscience. That is, it was a license for reformed Christians to believe what they felt honestly to be true, even if this went against the teachings of organized religion.

Church and State

Most reformers did not want disorder or anarchy within their Churches or within the state. From Luther onward, they called on local rulers to protect reformed preachers and their congregations and to encourage the spread of reformed ideas. In return, they instructed their congregations to obey lawful rulers and to be good citizens, taking their full share of civic responsibilities. Unlike Catholic religious leaders, who claimed superior, spiritual authority over all lay people, the early reformers (especially Luther) taught, in theory, that there should be a clear division between Church and state. In practice, this proved impossible, and reformers increasingly came to recognize rulers as chief members of the Church with a duty to impose reform and to punish or correct individuals who had broken the reformed Churches' ethical or religious laws.

John Frederick the Magnanimous (1503–1554), ruler of the German state of Saxony, encouraged Lutheranism within his lands and was its protector and benefactor.

Godly Magistrates

State magistrates often became responsible for punishing people accused of, for example, sexual immorality or spreading false Bible teachings, as well as secular crimes like theft or burglary. There was also considerable overlap of personnel between office-holders in Church and state. Presbyterian Church elders often served as city council members or local magistrates; their opinions and judgments were important in imposing discipline and making policy in secular and Church governing bodies. They were usually members of the most prosperous groups in society, with a vested interest in maintaining political stability and the economic status quo.

Breaking Away

Sometimes, however, the mutually supportive coalition between Church and state broke down. This might happen for several reasons. First, breakdown might occur if reformers considered a ruler unlawful for doctrinal or political reasons. A second reason might be if a ruler felt threatened by powerful cliques within the reformed Church—as happened, for example, in Scotland, where national synods (meetings) of Presbyterian Church elders seemed likely to set up a rival (and better organized) system of authority to the politically unsettled state. Third, conflict could occur if groups of reformed men and women decided, like the Anabaptists, that it was against their conscience to live in a particular society, either because it did not conform to their idea of godliness or because it did not allow them to live and worship in the way they chose.

Across Europe, many thousands of religious refugees, such as the Huguenots (French Protestants) who moved to England, left their homeland to settle in a country where the state-sponsored religion matched their own. Others left England, where they had been prosecuted as separatists (people who wanted to worship in their own congregations, apart from the rest of the community) to found new communities—for example, in 1620 the Mayflower Pilgrims founded a new settlement in America based on their religious beliefs.

This rather romantic 19th-century image shows the Mayflower Pilgrims arriving in America, full of thankfulness, in 1620.

A Difficult Issue

The reformers' vision of a godly Christian community proved surprisingly complicated to realize in practical terms. This was because it touched on several very delicate areas of 16th- and 17th-century life: the legitimacy (or otherwise) of rulers' claims to power, the maintenance of law and order, the enforcement of approved reformed belief, and the toleration or suppression of conflicting religious views. There were also questions of how the reformed Churches should be governed, and by whom, and how much right ordinary people had to express their individual, and maybe idiosyncratic, religious opinions.

Free Speech?

Looking back, it can sometimes seem difficult to imagine a world in which people were not free to think as they chose about religion and a religious lifestyle, or to express those views publicly. In some countries it could be dangerous even to discuss alternative ways of organizing society, however closely any new political system might be linked to approved religious beliefs. Actually putting new political ideas into practice, like the Mayflower Pilgrims or various radical groups during the English Civil War, was about equal to open rebellion against the government in power. Those who did so could not expect much support from the majority of reformed Church ministers or their congregations. Yet some bold—or foolhardy—Protestant groups continued to do this throughout the 17th and 18th centuries.

A few English examples illustrate what many were trying to achieve. The Diggers set up a community

The Amish are a Protestant group that originated in Switzerland and is now settled in Canada and the United States. Amish teach strict separation from the world and must live a simple life without modern technology.

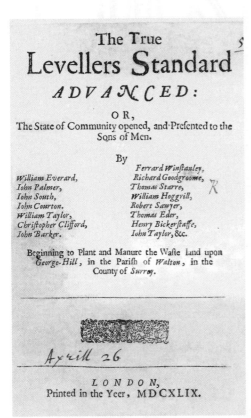

The Levellers hoped to create communal farms and gardens. In this pamphlet, published in 1649, they explained their plan to plant and fertilize the wasteland in the village of Walton in Surrey, England.

farming enterprise in 1649 in which each man was treated as an equal member of a fellowship, with no distinction of rank or wealth. The Levellers campaigned for radical social reform and votes for all adult men (except servants). The Ranters (always a tiny group) engaged in displays of public indecency, such as swearing and removing all their clothes to demonstrate their contempt for state and for organized Church laws.

Social Action

Even if, by present-day standards, law-abiding members and ministers of the first reformed Church congregations did not enjoy full freedom of speech or thought, their habits of direct prayer and independent Bible study marked a very significant change from older Catholic traditions. Combined with the reformers' insistence that Church members should fully participate in the running of the lawful state, it also marked the beginning of a custom of social comment and criticism, and sometimes action, among Protestant Churches that still continues today. During the 1960s, for example, American Protestant leaders such as the Reverend Dr. Martin Luther King, Jr., played a leading part in the civil rights movement, which called for equal treatment by the state and society for all American citizens regardless of their ethnic origins. As all reformed Christians knew, the Bible taught that everyone was equal in the sight of God.

Martin Luther King, Jr., founded the Southern Christian Leadership Conference with other black ministers in 1957 to promote the non-violent struggle against racism. Luther delivered his famous "I Have a Dream" speech during the March on Washington in 1963. The speech drew on Old Testament prophets and Christian images of brotherhood.

PART III: THE LEGACY

CHRISTIAN EUROPE DIVIDED

Reformation Failure?

The first reformers hoped to create a new generation of believers who understood Protestant teachings and actively lived them out. They had imagined that, once people heard the "truth," they would hurry to support the cause of reform. But this didn't happen as quickly or as thoroughly as they had hoped. Europe remained divided—a patchwork of Catholic and Protestant states (see map below). Many reformers, including Luther himself at times, felt discouraged. Had their efforts failed? What had gone wrong?

In many ways, nothing had gone wrong at all. Reform was taking place, but it was turning out to be a long, slow, and incomplete process, rather than a single, sudden

A map showing the religious divisions in Europe, 1650.

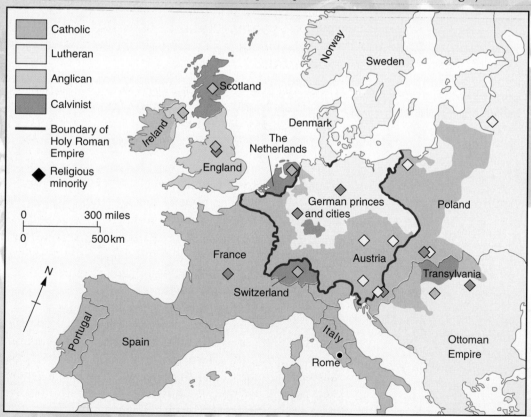

Henry of Navarre takes part in the sacrament of mass on becoming a Catholic, July 1593.

event. It was easy to see that religious change and politics would become so entangled they would be difficult to separate. This sometimes helped reform, but could also hinder or halt it. For example, Catholic rulers like Philip of Spain (reigned 1556–1598) felt obliged to become champions of the traditional Church, totally excluding Protestant ideas from their lands. In France, leading Protestant sympathizer Henry of Navarre changed his religious affiliation and became Catholic in 1593 so that he could be crowned king, famously commenting:

> *Paris is well worth a mass.*

Political struggles, including some horrific wars (see page 58), also turned people's minds away from the religious content of reform.

Misunderstanding

Reformers were also unrealistic in expecting ordinary people to grasp sophisticated religious arguments right away. Over 100 years after Luther made his first calls for Church reform, an English Protestant minister complained,

> *A man may preach long enough to hundreds in a congregation… who will not be able to give any accompt [account] of one sentence they hear, if they live a hundred years….It is almost incredible what strange conceits most ignorant people have of common notions….*

At a deeper psychological level, the reformers' ideas of salvation introduced a major change in the way people saw their world. They could no longer free themselves from sin through magical rituals. Instead, they had to be active in adopting a new lifestyle, based on private prayer, worship, study, and individual ethical choice. This was difficult for many to do.

At a more ordinary level, the successful practice of the Protestant religion required people to be literate. Yet less than half the population of Europe could read, and fewer still could afford to purchase Protestant texts. Moreover, until the 17th century, there was a serious shortage of trained, enthusiastic Protestant ministers who could preach and teach reform.

The Counter-Reformation

There was another reason why reform failed in certain European countries. Simultaneously, the Catholic Church had launched a reform initiative of its own to remove abuses and corruption and, later, to fight against the spread of Protestant ideas. This process, called the Counter-Reformation by historians, sprang from many of the same 15th-century Catholic roots as Luther's own calls for reform, and had many of the same aims. But it grew to become a much larger movement that, between 1550 and 1650, transformed the Catholic Church.

Monks and Missionaries

The Counter-Reformation was launched at Catholic Church Councils, held at Trent in the Alps, between 1545 and 1563. The Councils' leaders called for an end to political divisions and theological quarrels within the Church, for a renewal of faith and piety among priests and people, for a revival of ancient monastic traditions,

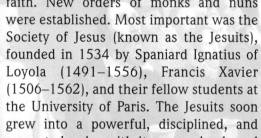

St. Ignatius of Loyola (kneeling, right) presents the rule book of the newly founded Jesuit order to Pope Paul III.

and for fresh missionary activities. The latter would make sure existing Catholics truly understood key Catholic beliefs, and would win new converts for the Catholic faith. New orders of monks and nuns were established. Most important was the Society of Jesus (known as the Jesuits), founded in 1534 by Spaniard Ignatius of Loyola (1491–1556), Francis Xavier (1506–1562), and their fellow students at the University of Paris. The Jesuits soon grew into a powerful, disciplined, and respected order with its own schools and universities and a formidable reputation for preaching and winning converts. In 1540 Francis Xavier embarked on a remarkable series of overseas journeys, attempting to spread the Catholic faith in India, China, and Japan.

Positive and Negative

To encourage devotion—and emphasize the Church's spiritual authority—Catholic Church leaders, rulers, and other powerful people who supported them founded new schools, colleges, and universities, and commissioned many magnificent works of art,

The high altar, baldacchino (canopy), and papal throne in St. Peter's Basilica, Rome, were designed by Italian sculptor Bernini (1598–1686). They are examples of the superb works of art completed during the Counter-Reformation era.

These Spanish heretics are being burned in brick kilns by the Inquisition, while a Catholic priest (top left) prays.

architecture, literature, and church music in expressive, emotional styles. But they also supported movements to suppress religious or philosophical ideas that criticized, or appeared to threaten, the teachings of the Catholic Church. In particular, they encouraged the work of a feared and often hated Church institution—the Inquisition. Originally founded in the 13th century as a Catholic Church court with very wide powers, including torture, the Inquisition was intended to investigate and stamp out heresy. Local branches of the Inquisition could be set up in individual countries to meet a particular need. In Italy, for example, the brilliant scientist Galileo Galilei (1564–1642) was imprisoned after being tried by the Inquisition for daring to suggest that the Earth orbited the Sun (traditionally, Catholic scholars believed that the Earth must be the center of God's creation). More tragically, in Spain, the local Inquisition (founded 1478–1480) combined religious persecution of Protestants (over 2,000 were executed and 15,000 received lesser punishments) with a genocidal hatred of religious and ethnic minority groups (mostly Muslims and Jews) who had been peacefully settled in Spain for hundreds of years.

Authority

Like the Protestant reform movement, the Counter-Reformation could not remain separate from politics. Within the Catholic Church itself, this led to demands for absolute loyalty to the Pope as the supreme authority in Catholic Church government and doctrine, and to priests as guardians of parishioners' souls. It also led to uncritical Church support for Catholic rulers—especially the powerful kings of Spain—as "defenders of the faith."

England—A Special Case

After 1550, the Church in England was separated organizationally and doctrinally not only from the traditional Catholic Church, but also from all other reformed Churches in Europe. With a monarch as its supreme governor, a mildly Protestant set of religious teachings, but a Catholic-style hierarchy of bishops and archbishops, it was unique and extraordinary. Henry VIII had claimed (and probably genuinely believed) that royal leadership of the Church was ordained by God. Subsequent English kings and queens did not all share his view but, for at least the next 200 years, they all wanted to influence Church government and control relations between Church and state.

Tensions

At the same time, the stability of the Elizabethan religious compromise was strained by groups of radical Protestants, including Puritans and Dissenters. The Puritans were Calvinist Presbyterians who influenced the anti-monarchist government led by Oliver Cromwell between 1653 and 1658. Cromwell's parliaments abolished bishops and the established Church of England Prayer Book, but both were reintroduced after Charles II restored the monarchy in 1660. Dissenters refused to accept them, however, and broke away from the state-established Church to found new sects on their own. This was against the law and led to repeated clashes between governments and Dissenting groups.

Protestants Only

There were quarrels between moderate Protestants and High-Church bishops who wanted to emphasize continuing links with the pre-reform Catholic Church in England. There were also disputes between kings (like James II, reigned 1685–1688, who secretly became Catholic) and parliaments over who had the power to suspend or dispense with laws governing religious tolerance and the administration of the Church. In 1689 the Bill of Rights attempted to halt any further Catholic influence by insisting that only a Protestant heir might succeed to the throne. This law was further strengthened by the Act of Settlement in 1701, which stated that non-Protestants could not become king or queen, even if they had the best legal claim to inherit the crown.

Just a Formality?

Ever since then, the ruling British monarch must be Protestant, and is still head of the Church in England. Church of England bishops still sit in Parliament, with the power to vote for or against government legislation. By the 20th century, with its increasingly secular outlook, these links between Church and state might have seemed just a formality, but they had dramatic political and personal consequences on more than one occasion. In 1936 King Edward VIII gave up the throne, amid great scandal, to marry a divorced woman. Then, the Church of England taught that divorced people should not re-marry while their former spouses were alive, and many felt that it was undesirable for the King, as head of the Church, to flout its religious laws.

In the late 1990s, religious leaders and constitutional experts discussed whether heir to the throne Prince Charles, a Protestant widower, should be allowed to marry Camilla Parker-Bowles, who was a Catholic divorcee. In secular law, the couple were perfectly free to wed, but some leaders of the Church of England still questioned their right to marry in the eyes of God. For historical, political, and religious reasons—or perhaps through prejudice—some British people also expressed reluctance to see a Catholic as queen.

The links between Church and state in England remained politically important for centuries. The abdication of King Edward VIII in 1936 to marry Mrs. Wallis Simpson, an American divorcee, was headline-news worldwide.

Oxford Mail

No. 2,407.   TELEPHONE 4141.   THURSDAY, 10 DECEMBER, 1936.   PRICE ONE PENNY.

KING EDWARD ABDICATES
Dramatic Message Read To Parliament

"FINAL AND IRREVOCABLE DECISION"

CAN NO LONGER DISCHARGE THIS HEAVY TASK

DUKE OF YORK NEW MONARCH

IN A DENSELY PACKED HOUSE OF COMMONS THIS AFTERNOON THE SPEAKER ANNOUNCED KING EDWARD'S DECISION TO ABDICATE AND THE DUKE OF YORK'S SUCCESSION TO THE THRONE.

THE PRIME MINISTER HANDED THE FOLLOWING MESSAGE TO THE SPEAKER, AND THE SPEAKER THEN READ IT TO THE HOUSE:—

"After long and anxious consideration, I have determined to renounce the Throne, to which I succeeded on the death of my father, and I am now communicating this, my final and irrevocable decision.

King Edward.

COMMONS PACKED FOR DRAMATIC SCENE

MRS. SIMPSON WILL NOT LEAVE CANNES

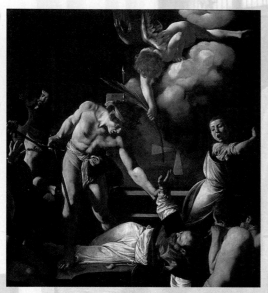 

Contemporary art styles reflected the differences in Catholic and Protestant worldviews. Compare the dark, brooding picture of the martyrdom of St. Matthew (left) by Italian artist Caravaggio (1571–1610) with the simple, devout woman who symbolizes "Faith" in the painting (right) by Dutch artist Jan Vermeer (c.1632–1675).

Europe Divided

The slow, partial process of reform meant that Europe became—and stayed—divided along religious as well as political lines. These divisions remained substantially the same until the 20th century, when people became more skeptical—or apathetic—toward Christian beliefs. Over the years they contributed to a widening cultural divide, accompanied by hostility, or at least suspicion, between the mainly Protestant north and the predominantly Catholic south. Where these larger religious divisions were mirrored within a single location, like Ireland, there were often tragic results.

European religious divisions were reinforced by two very different processes—the international movement for Catholic renewal known today as the Counter-Reformation, and the efforts of ruling monarchs to maintain control of, or at least guide, all Church activities within their lands. Few achieved this so successfully as the kings and queens of England, whose actions created an official, national Church. The reformed Church in England became the Church of England, sometimes known as the Anglican Church, closely linked to the monarch as head of state, and with the right to take part in national government.

Rivalry and Identity

Differences between Catholic and Protestant countries did not incite rivalries between European states, or cause the growing sense of national identity and, sometimes, isolationism that was developing among the countries of Europe. These were happening anyway, for a complex variety of political and economic reasons. But religious differences did, at times, contribute to them—for example in Spain, where the inward-looking institutions of the Counter-Reformation seemed aimed at creating a nation of soldiers and ecclesiastics in great contrast to the outgoing, trade-based, profit-minded society of the Calvinist Netherlands. These generalizations hide many local variations—there were busy Spanish merchants, and contemplative, spiritual, people in many Protestant lands. But travelers across Europe remarked on the increasingly striking differences between nations.

European Churches Overseas

Through the efforts of Catholic and, later, Protestant missionaries, the European religious divide was also exported worldwide. Until the 18th century, the Catholic countries of southern Europe, especially Spain and Portugal, ruled the largest overseas empires, where they promoted the work of Catholic missionaries. During the later 18th and 19th centuries, Protestant countries in northern Europe, especially Great Britain and the Netherlands, took control of vast regions in Asia and Africa, and encouraged the spread of the Protestant faith there. The effects of these colonial missions can still be observed today. Many lands once ruled by Spain and Portugal, especially in Central and South America and the Philippines, remain Catholic, and there are Anglican Churches in Australia, Canada, New Zealand, South Africa, and other lands formerly controlled by the British Empire.

In 1667, these two Jesuit missionaries in China were part of the Counter-Reformation's huge missionary initiative to bring Catholicism to not only China but India and the Americas, as well.

TROUBLE AND STRIFE

Religious Rivals

Although religious differences between nations did not, by themselves, usually lead to war, religious quarrels between political rivals within one nation often did cause conflict. In 16th-century France, for example, there was almost 40 years of intermittent fighting in which religious intolerance and persecution played an important part. For this reason, the events of 1562–1598 are often known as the French Wars of Religion.

However, the underlying motive for the French wars was not religious, but dynastic. By the mid-16th century, the Valois family of kings, who had ruled France since 1328, was losing its grasp on political power. Valois King Henry II died in 1559, leaving four sons, all too young or too feeble to rule alone, and three rival noble families, all eager to seize power. One, the Guise (who had married into the royal family), were Catholic; their enemies, the Bourbon and the (more moderate) Montmerency, were Protestant. The Bourbon, in particular, were supported by the many small, local Protestant churches that had been set up in France by supporters of Calvin's teachings. Unlike Protestants in England or Germany, they were not controlled by powerful rulers or city councils; some were prepared to use violence and other forms of lawlessness to further Protestant reform. Concerned by this threat to public order, and continuing the Valois' kings generally hostile policy toward reform, in 1562 the Guise ordered the massacre of 74 Protestants at a church service.

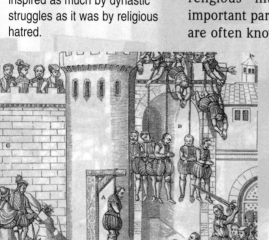

The massacre of Protestants at Amboise, France, in 1562. Persecution such as this was inspired as much by dynastic struggles as it was by religious hatred.

More Massacres

From then on, there were countless acts of violence between Catholic and Protestant nobles and their supporters. The most brutal was in 1572, when the Guise family plotted the assassination of the head of the Montmerency family. On St. Bartholomew's Day, he was

Catholic soldiers attacked thousands of French Protestants during the infamous St. Bartholomew's Day Massacre in 1572.

The most famous English Catholic conspiracy was that of Guy Fawkes (1570–1605), who plotted to blow up Parliament in 1605. His plot was discovered (or, probably, betrayed) and he was executed.

killed, together with thousands of Protestants who had come to Paris to celebrate the wedding of the leading Bourbon, Henry of Navarre.

In the next few days, around 30,000 Protestants were massacred across France. After this, fighting between Catholics and Protestants intensified, and combined with many other national and local quarrels. Many Protestants began to talk about revolutionary political theories such as republicanism. They no longer felt bound to obey rulers who sanctioned attacks on their subjects. From 1585–1589, there was outright war as an alliance of Catholic nobles, known as the Holy League and backed by Spain, tried to prevent Protestant Henry of Navarre from inheriting the French crown. Henry won, but peace was finally achieved only after he agreed to become Catholic (see page 51). However, in 1598, he passed the Edict of Nantes, allowing all French Protestants limited freedom to worship as they chose.

The Low Countries and Britain

Around the same time as the French wars, religious differences in the Low Countries (now Belgium and the Netherlands, but at that time ruled by Spain) combined with movements for political independence to start a rebellion, which created two new, separate states. In England there were plots by Catholics against Protestant rulers. Until 1587 these focused on Mary Queen of Scots (the daughter of a Guise mother and widow of Valois King Francis II), who was the nearest Catholic heir to the English throne. After Mary's execution, groups of Catholic noblemen continued to plan conspiracies.

A particularly intolerant series of witch trials took place in the Protestant community of Salem, Massachusetts, in 1692. This overdramatized view of the trials was made in 1883.

Intolerance

The sense of religious and social disorientation brought about by rapid religious change in the 16th and 17th centuries also contributed to destructive social phenomena, ranging from suspicion and intolerance among neighbors to witch hunts and large-scale executions. The polarization of religious loyalties, especially when accompanied by persecution, encouraged attacks on non-conformists. People also searched for scapegoats to explain their growing sense of personal unease. Historians estimate that over 40,000 alleged witches were killed in Europe between 1500 and 1700.

Magic and Misfortunes

Looking back, these figures appear surprising—at least to begin with. A belief in witches was nothing new. It was widespread in medieval Europe, and witchcraft was strongly condemned by the Catholic Church. But medieval accusations of witchcraft were rare, and led to few investigations or prosecutions. This was partly because witchcraft fit in well with the pre-reform view of the world, which relied on the performance of magical rituals, like the mass, to establish links between man and God.

It was also because traditional Catholic teachings interpreted misfortunes (of the kind later attributed to witchcraft) as the result of personal wickedness or original sin. They were a punishment for bad behavior, and could be cured or eased by sacraments like confession and penance. Reformers interpreted misfortune, pain, and suffering in a rather different way. They were not necessarily the consequences of personal or communal sin, but might be caused by the Devil and his helpers—witches—at work in the world. These constantly tempted Christians to stray from godly living. As a consequence, people became increasingly conscious of witchcraft and perceived it to be far more dangerous.

Social Tensions

Historians today have suggested another reason why accusations of witchcraft increased so rapidly during the early years of reform. The 16th century was also a time of economic crisis and social change. Old community ways of working, in shared open fields, for example, were being replaced by wage labor for rich landlords. There was often unemployment and hunger. Old community institutions (some based in churches), which encouraged people to help their neighbors, were also breaking down. People trusted one another less; poor people were angry with, and envious of, the rich, while the wealthy accused the poor of laziness and law-breaking. In this antagonistic atmosphere, quarrels between neighbors, especially between the poor and more wealthy villagers, easily became inflamed.

Men and women who quarreled with local communities could be locked in a stock, where they were pelted with rotten food.

The Weaker Sex?

People accused of witchcraft could be Catholic or Protestant, but most of them were women. This is partly because women were the poorest members of society. Without family or friends to help them, it was very difficult for women to survive, especially if they were old or ill. If an elderly woman went begging, stole food, or offered to sell traditional herbal remedies and magic charms, she could be perceived as a threat to the local community's material or spiritual health.

The execution of three alleged witches in the Harz Mountains, Germany, in 1555.

However, this was not how some 16th-century witch hunters saw women. Their explanations for female deviancy ranged from suggesting that women were feebler in mind and body than men—and so more liable to be tempted by the Devil—to women's terrible temper. This meant that it was:

 not possible for them to control themselves. Like brute beasts, they fix their furious eye on the person whom they believe has done them wrong, and they bewitch them.

Religious Power

Awareness of religious feelings was an essential element of government policy throughout Europe during the 16th and 17th centuries. Sometimes it involved little more than a strong-minded resolve to resist all opposing religious ideas. But often it was more sophisticated and complicated. Political differences within nations could be useful to rulers who were pursuing policies of conquest or control. They could also be cynically manipulated to weaken an enemy state or to help bring a rebellious province under control. When combined with aggressive religious convictions, they could sometimes be devastating, as the example of British government involvement in Ireland in the 16th and 17th centuries demonstrates.

Plantations

English monarchs had claimed the right to control Ireland ever since 1169, although Irish chiefs had frequently rebelled. Henry VIII pursued a policy of conciliation toward them, but his ministers (with his approval) tried to introduce English-style administrative reforms in both the Irish Catholic Church and the state. Irish chiefs and people did not support these foreign ideas, and resented English attempts to enforce them. Alarmed by the threat of riot and rebellion, Mary I (ironically, a Catholic) introduced a new policy of "plantation."

Mary's policies were inspired by the example of new Spanish colonial settlements in America. They were followed by Elizabeth I (ruled 1558–1603), James I (1603–1625), and Charles I (1625–1649). All wanted an increased English, Protestant presence in Ireland for fear that the Catholic Irish would support England's Catholic enemies, France and (after Mary's death) Spain. Plantations aimed at virtual ethnic cleansing. Native Irish chiefs and ordinary people, all mostly Catholic, were driven from their lands by Protestant settlers from England and lowland Scotland. Beginning in 1609, large numbers of Scots settled in the ancient Irish kingdom of Ulster in the north.

Rebellion and War

In 1641 the Irish people rebelled, massacring English and Scottish settlers. There were further atrocities on both sides during the battles that followed, when Irish

The Battle of the Boyne was the decisive battle in the struggle for control of Ireland. Its anniversary is still celebrated by Irish Protestants.

Puritan sympathizer Oliver Cromwell (1599–1658) believed he was fighting on the side of God.

nationalists fought in a three-cornered struggle against rival armies supporting Royalist and Parliamentarian sides during the English Civil War. In 1649–1650 the Parliamentarian commander, Oliver Cromwell, became famous (or infamous) for his ruthless tactics, especially at the battles of Drogheda and Wexford.

After the Battle of the Boyne in 1690, when Protestant Dutch King William III (who had married English Queen Mary II) defeated an Irish Catholic army, laws were passed to give Protestants control of all areas of Irish life. Catholics were banned from Parliament, the law, universities, and the navy. They could not vote, run a school, or own valuable property, and it was very difficult for them to inherit land. In 1603 Catholic chiefs and ordinary farmers owned 90 percent of Ireland; in 1641 they owned 60 percent; by 1659 this had dropped to only 10 percent. Catholic bishops were driven out of Ireland, and only a few other Catholic priests were allowed under license from the English government.

Tragically, Cromwell, like many other Catholic and Protestant soldiers who fought in Ireland, was deeply sincere, and felt that he was acting for his country's good. In a report to Parliament in London, he justified his actions at Drogheda as:

 God's judgment on a bloodthirsty and barbarous enemy.

Since Cromwell's time, rival groups of Catholics and Protestants have, sincerely or cynically, used religious differences to justify horrific acts of violence. The Irish "Troubles" still continue today.

Religion as an Excuse

Conflicts like the French Wars of Religion or the Thirty Years War, which was fought between rival German princes and their international supporters from 1618 to 1648, were not caused by religious differences. In all of them, however, religious quarrels provided an ideological justification for fighting, and often led to increased feelings of hostility among soldiers and civilians on opposite sides of political arguments. To many, it seemed easier to kill an enemy for a godly cause, or to persecute them if they could be labeled as agents of the Devil (like witches) or as enemies of the one true faith.

During the Thirty Years War (1618–1648), religious differences among German states tragically led to involvement in a wider conflict between rival European powers.

The 16th and 17th centuries were also times of great intolerance, when religious faith, social inadequacy (which made people outcasts in their community), or simple, ignorant superstition, could literally be a matter of life and death. Often, the only safety lay in conformity with the beliefs or prejudices of people in power. Nonconformists faced social ostracism and, like 17th-century Irish Catholics, suffered the loss of land and civil rights. Some, like the Huguenots in France, had to choose between exile or the forced acceptance of beliefs they did not hold. Others fled abroad, many to America, seeking religious freedom, or at least acceptance, in a new, more tolerant land.

Religion and Identity

In Ireland and elsewhere, religious differences also became linked to questions of tribal or regional identity. Fighting for "the faith" became part of a larger struggle to preserve traditional culture in all its forms and, often, to remove a hated foreign overlord. With such huge issues at stake, martyrs on both sides could easily be created, adding an extra dimension to a national history based on tales of oppression and injustice. In this context, failure to support a national religion became an

Members of the Portadown lodge of the Orange Order march from Drumcree church to the roadblock that prevents them from completing their march down the nationalist Garvaghy Road. In the late 1990s, Protestant and Catholic groups in Northern Ireland have repeatedly failed to agree over the route for the annual Orange Order march.

act of disloyalty and betrayal. This was true even when fighters on both sides had no sincerely held personal faith.

Freedom or License?

As we saw earlier, the idea of freedom of conscience did exist, in a limited way, during the early years of religious reform, though it was often not put into practice. Today it is much more widespread, and is valued by many people who have no formal religious beliefs of their own. Its supporters hope that it might bring an end to centuries of conflict triggered by religious and tribal differences. But recent events in Northern Ireland and the Middle East have proved this is not always so. A terrible dilemma, therefore, confronts many people of goodwill. Do they support religious freedom and, with it, a tiny minority of terrorists willing to use religion to justify violent ends? Or do they abandon their belief in tolerance, and limit the freedom of people who hold extreme or unpopular religious or political views?

NOW AND THEN

Many New Churches

As we have seen, many new Churches were founded as a result of 16th-century calls for religious reform. Some of these, like the Church of England, were closely linked to, and strictly controlled by, national governments. Others, like the Protestant Churches based on the teachings of reformers Luther and Calvin, grew up in many different European nations, where they developed to meet local spiritual and social needs and adapted to local political conditions. A few, like the Anabaptist communities of Central Europe, survived persecution and remained resolutely separate from all other religious or secular authorities.

In many Catholic nations, no Protestant Churches were tolerated; even in some Protestant countries, only one reformed Church was allowed. In England, for example, all Dissenting (or nonconformist) Churches were banned by the Act of Uniformity of 1662, for mainly political reasons. (Dissenters had fought against the King during the English Civil War.) This ban was relaxed slightly by the Toleration Act of 1689, but even so, members of nonconformist churches could not hold municipal or state office until 1828 (nor could Catholics until 1829). But this did not stop new Protestant Churches from forming and attracting many members. In England, these included Baptists, Independents or Congregationalists, and Quakers (see page 68), all founded in the 16th and 17th centuries; Methodists, founded by Charles and John Wesley in the 18th century; and the Salvation Army, founded by William Booth in the 19th century. A census taken in England in 1851 showed that there were almost as many nonconformists as members of the established (Anglican) Church of England. By 1900 there were more nonconformists than Anglicans. Nonconformist Churches were especially popular in working-class districts.

Methodist leader John Wesley (1703–1791) attracted vast crowds to hear his sermons, which he often preached

All these new reformed Churches were seeking what they hoped would be the best way to worship God. This did not stop them from fiercely criticizing the established Church of England and, sometimes, quarreling bitterly among themselves. They all shared similar core beliefs centered on Luther's concept of salvation through faith and a personal commitment to a godly way of life, but their patterns of worship and their organizational structures differed considerably. Some chose simple prayers and psalms, or even silence, for their worship; others included exuberant music and lively dancing in their services. Most were led by powerful preachers, who guided Church members' personal and communal lives.

From the 17th century onward, members of all the different European Protestant Churches traveled as merchants, settlers, and missionaries to many other parts of the world, taking their own preferred style of worship and Church with them. Everywhere, these transplanted Churches were influenced by ancient local traditions or the settlers' own pioneering social ideas. New, local forms of European Protestant Churches developed, together with American, Caribbean, African, and Asian Churches that preached the message of reformed Christianity in a new way. The reformed, Protestant tradition now has many more members, and is more active outside Europe than within Europe where it began.

Ecstatic singing at a Sunday service in South America.

Equal in the Sight of God

The earliest reformers taught that, spiritually speaking, all Christian men and women were equal in the sight of God, and could communicate directly with him through prayer. They also taught that all members of Christian congregations had a duty to live out their faith in their daily lives. These teachings had two important consequences. First, ways of worship in reformed Churches tended to be plain and simple, emphasizing the importance of personal prayer and the study of God's Word in the Bible. Second, from the 17th to the 19th centuries, these teachings also led many (though not all) Protestant Churches to play an active part in liberal politics, campaigning on behalf of poor and oppressed peoples. Politically, they became linked with parties that supported individual liberty, institutions with elected representatives, social progress, and a limited role for the state.

Both these tendencies were most clearly demonstrated by a Protestant group known as the Society of Friends, or the Quakers. The Society was founded formally by English Protestant George Fox and others in 1667, though they had met together for worship some time before then. Their nickname came from Fox urging his friends to:

 quake at the Word of the Lord.

Fox and the other Quakers believed that men and women possessed an inner light of conscience or spiritual awareness that enabled them to experience God's Holy Spirit at work, guiding their lives. To worship, they met together in silence until the Spirit moved them to speak.

Quakers aimed to live simply, and had no priests, formal prayers, or organized church services. They addressed one another as brother or sister, refusing to acknowledge titles of rank that suggested that some people were more important than others. The Quakers faced persecution in England, and many left to settle in America, where they established a new colony in Pennsylvania in 1682. Since then, groups of Quakers worldwide have been active in political and social

This image of an American Quaker prayer meeting in 1744 shows the informality and simplicity of Quaker worship.

At the Truth and Reconciliation Commission in May 1997, Archbishop Desmond Tutu greets the family and friends of children shot dead by South African police.

Jubilee 2000 campaigners, many of whom are Christians, attend a rally in London in December 2000, calling for increased action to reduce the burden of debt in third world countries.

campaigns, and are especially concerned with issues of tolerance, justice, and peace.

Members of Protestant Churches also played an important part in many 19th-century social campaigns, especially the movement to outlaw slavery led by William Wilberforce, as well as the British legislative program to improve conditions for women and children in factories and mines, steered through Parliament by the Earl of Shaftesbury. Both Wilberforce and Shaftesbury were members of the Evangelical movement—an informal association of mostly nonconformist Christians who stressed the need for personal moral rebirth, intensive Bible study, and social reform. In 20th-century America, Protestant ministers like Martin Luther King, Jr., continued this tradition and became leading figures in the civil rights movement, which aimed to end racial segregation and discrimination throughout the United States.

By the late 20th century, members of many socially more conservative Churches, including the Church of England and the Roman Catholic Church, also decided to join in the nonconformist tradition of action for radical political and social reform. In South America, senior Roman Catholic priests worked to restore democracy in countries ruled by oppressive regimes. In South Africa, Anglican Archbishop Desmond Tutu was a leading campaigner against apartheid, and led the astonishing Truth and Reconciliation Commission, which attempted to bring peace and healing to families and communities traumatized by violence during the apartheid years. More recently, members of many different Churches took part in the Jubilee 2000 campaign, which called for a cancellation of debts owed by poor countries to richer ones. The campaign continues today.

New Words, New Music

The central importance of the Bible text and of individual Bible study to Protestant Churches had an enormous cultural impact, both in words and in music. This was most powerful in Europe and America, from the 17th to the early 20th centuries, but still persists today in many parts of the world. The words of the Bible influenced everything from personal names to the development of what many considered to be the best, or most correct, style of writing formal English prose. The Bible was also used as a physical touchstone to denote good faith. In many countries, people giving evidence or swearing an oath traditionally place their hands on a copy of the Bible to show that they are speaking the truth.

Names, Language, Stories, and Study

From the late 16th century onward, names that commemorated remarkable characters in Bible stories (from Adam to Zebedee), or praised spiritual virtues described by writers of the New Testament, such as Hope, Faith, and Joy, became popular throughout Protestant lands. In contrast, most Catholic parents preferred to name their children after Catholic saints.

This embroidered sampler was made in 1839 by Elizabeth Lyon. It features verses from the Bible and an image of Adam and Eve (top).

The translation of the Bible (completed 1604–1611) authorized by King James I was the most widely read book in England for centuries. Its solemn but beautiful language was held up as an example for all readers and writers to learn from. Many of its phrases, such as "from strength to strength," "at death's door," and "fight the good fight," entered everyday English speech. Bible texts were printed and sold cheaply to be displayed in ordinary families' homes, or were patiently embroidered by many women on samplers and wall-hangings. Today, this tradition is continued by poster campaigns paid for by Protestant missionary organizations, and on placards with eye-catching slogans outside many Protestant Churches.

Parents read regularly to children from the Bible and sent them to Sunday schools, where they were taught Bible stories and encouraged to learn passages from the Bible by heart. Groups of adults met together to study and discuss Bible texts, and scholars labored over ancient Greek, Hebrew, and Aramaic manuscripts to produce new and more accurate Bible translations, or versions of Bible stories written in simple language that everyone could understand.

Spiritual Sounds

In music, Bible texts inspired many great works, including Passions and Oratorios (Bible passages telling the story of Jesus' life and death, sung by soloists and choirs) written by 18th-century European classical composers J.S. Bach and G.F. Handel. The Messiah, Handel's masterpiece, with its rousing Hallelujah Chorus, is still very popular today. Protestant writers, especially the Methodist Charles Wesley, also composed a great many hymns based on Bible texts. In America, Bible words and stories formed the inspiration for many spirituals (powerfully moving songs of faith and suffering that gave hope to African-American slaves) and 20th-century Gospel music. Today, there is still a great tradition of music-making in many reformed Churches worldwide.

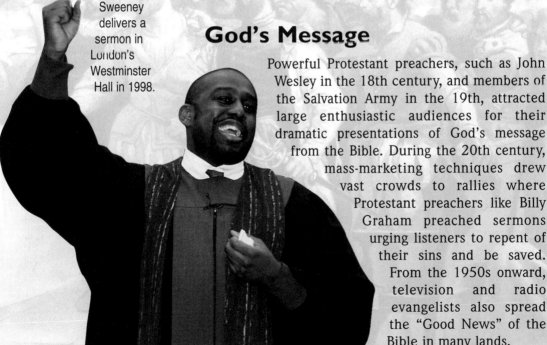

Charismatic Protestant preachers, gospel singers, and evangelists still attract large audiences today, especially in the United States. Here, the Reverend Ian Sweeney delivers a sermon in London's Westminster Hall in 1998.

God's Message

Powerful Protestant preachers, such as John Wesley in the 18th century, and members of the Salvation Army in the 19th, attracted large enthusiastic audiences for their dramatic presentations of God's message from the Bible. During the 20th century, mass-marketing techniques drew vast crowds to rallies where Protestant preachers like Billy Graham preached sermons urging listeners to repent of their sins and be saved. From the 1950s onward, television and radio evangelists also spread the "Good News" of the Bible in many lands.

71

Shaping Our World

The Reformation, or Reformations, began over 400 years ago, when people's ideas and lifestyles were very different from those of today. Yet although many 21st century men and women may or may not believe the message preached by the Protestant reformers (or any version of Christianity), they can still observe the results of the early reformers' thoughts, words, and deeds in the modern world.

Many reformed Churches still exist and play an active part (along with other religious organizations) in educational, cultural, and welfare programs. The words of the Bible, and music inspired by the Protestant faith, are still familiar to many people in English-speaking countries, even if they have never attended a Church service. Many political parties still acknowledge the importance of non-conformist Protestant ideas of social justice.

But the long process of Church reform started by 16th-century protesters achieved more than just new Churches, fine words and music, or a concern for equality. It also shattered the legal, administrative, and cultural unity of pre-16th century Catholic Europe, and introduced a new, more active model for each citizen's godly life. As it set up new links between reformed Churches and independent nation states, it contributed to—although it did not cause—the emergence of new political structures that shaped the modern world. By breaking away from international Catholic institutions, Church reform provided the opportunities for new, local ones to take their place, in everything from national and Church government to community and family life.

During the late 20th century, Christians from many different traditions began to meet, talk, and work together. Here, the Anglican Archbishop of Canterbury and Roman Catholic Pope John Paul II greet one another during a service at Canterbury Cathedral, England, in 1982.

altar a table or similar structure in a church, where mass, Holy Communion, or the Lord's Supper is celebrated

Anabaptists groups of radical Protestants who believed in adult re-baptism and set up separate communities to live apart from the rest of the world

Anglican another name for the Church of England

baptism a ritual that washed away original sin and made men, women, and children members of the Christian Church

catechism a series of questions designed to teach basic Christian beliefs

Catholic (or Roman Catholic) belonging to the Church headed by the Pope in Rome

chantry a special chapel where masses were said or sung by priests to free the souls of dead people from purgatory

Church of England the government-backed Church, with mainly Protestant beliefs but many elements of pre-Reformation Catholic structure, that was established by law in England during the 16th century. It was (and still is) headed by the ruling monarch

confirmation a ritual or sacrament that admits baptized Christians to full membership, and allows them to participate in mass or Holy Communion

commonwealth community

creeds formal statements of religious belief

Dissenters groups of people in England who refused to accept the religious settlement imposed by the government in 1660–1662, when the monarchy was restored. The settlement included bishops and archbishops to lead the Church of England, and the King James Prayer Book

doctrine religious teaching

dogma firmly held belief

Episcopal led by bishops and archbishops

extreme unction a ritual or sacrament to bless the dying

foreordained decided in advance (by God)

grace God's favor, or mercy, that saves Christians from the consequences of sin

heretics people who held religious views not approved by the Church or government in any particular state

High Church members of the Anglican Church (Church of England) who emphasize its links with the pre-Reformation Catholic Church

Holy Communion (also called the Lord's Supper) a sacrament that commemorates Jesus' last meal with his disciples, and his death to save humanity from sin

humanists scholars, thinkers, and artists who admired humanity's dignity and achievements, and valued human experience (in contrast with traditional Christian views of weak, sinful humankind)

idolatry the worship of idols (false gods)

indulgences documents issued by the pre-Reformation Catholic Church, which guaranteed to limit a soul's time in purgatory

justification a spiritual process of cleansing and rebirth—one of Martin Luther's key beliefs

Lollards the followers of John Wycliffe, a 14th-century campaigner for Catholic Church reform
Lord's Supper *see* **Holy Communion**

mass the most important sacrament in the Catholic Church, which mysteriously re-enacts Jesus' last meal with his disciples, and his death to save humanity from sin

nonconformist a Protestant Christian who did not accept either the beliefs or the ways of worship of the established Church of England

ordination the sacrament or ritual of becoming a priest
original sin the inborn wickedness of all humanity, resulting from Adam and Eve's disobedience to God

penance acts to atone for sins, such as prayer, fasting, or good works
predestination the belief that God has chosen some people to be saved from their sins—one of Jean Calvin's key ideas
Presbyterian led by ministers and elders, and supervised by elected representatives of church congregations
Protestant a Christian who followed the teachings of reformers who broke away from the Catholic Church during the 15th and 16th centuries (also, a member of non-Catholic Christian Churches today)

purgatory according to Catholic belief, a place where Christian souls go after death to be punished and purified before reaching heaven
Puritans groups of Calvinist Presbyterians in England who aimed to live simply and worship plainly. They opposed High Church beliefs and supported Parliament against Royalists in the English Civil War

relics the physical remains of holy men and women
Royalist a person who supported King Charles I in his fight against Parliament during the English Civil War. Most Royalists also supported the established Church of England

sacraments rituals leading to salvation
salvation being saved from sin to enjoy life after death in heaven
sanctuary the holiest part of a church building
superstitions beliefs that others think are irrational, illogical, or founded on mistaken views

transcendent linking humans with God, or another spiritual power
transubstantiated spiritually transformed
Trinity the three aspects of the Christian God: the Father, the Son (Jesus), and the Holy Spirit

TIMELINE OF EVENTS

1274	Catholic Church Councils start to call for reform
c.1325	Renaissance begins
c.1380s	Lollards begin to hold religious meetings
1419–33	Followers of Hus fight against German Catholic rulers
1455	Gutenberg prints Bible
1517	Luther lists 95 theses against indulgences
1518	Zwingli preaches in Switzerland
1521	Luther excommunicated. Henry VIII "Defender of the Faith"
1524–26	German Peasants' War
1529	Charles V ends religious toleration in his empire; German princes protest
1529–31	Swiss war of religion
1534	English Parliament passes Act of Supremacy
1534	Society of Jesus (Jesuits) founded
1536–40	Dissolution of the monasteries in England
1540	Catholic missionaries leave for Asia
1541	Calvin's Protestant commonwealth in Geneva
1545–63	Catholic Church Councils meet at Trent
1549	Book of Common Prayer
1554	Catholic worship and obedience to the Pope restored in England
1559	Elizabethan Settlement
1560	Presbyterianism becomes state religion of Scotland
1562–98	Wars of Religion in France
1572	St. Bartholomew's Day Massacre, France
1579	Protestant Northern Netherlands break with Catholic rule
1598	Edict of Nantes
1604–11	Authorized Version of Bible in English
1618–48	Thirty Years War
1620	Mayflower Pilgrims sail to America
1641	Catholic Irish rebel against English rule
1642–48	Civil War in England
1652	Quakers founded
1660	Monarchy restored in England
1688	Catholic James II replaced by Protestant William of Orange
1689	Bill of Rights
1690	Battle of the Boyne
1692	Salem, Mass. witch trials
1701	Act of Settlement
1828	Protestant non-conformists allowed to hold public office in Britain
1829	Catholics given equal rights with Protestants in Britain

BOOKS TO READ

There are many excellent books on the Reformation. The following are especially useful:

Cameron, Euan. *The European Reformation*. New York: Oxford University Press, 1995.

Cressy, David, and Lori Anne Ferrell (eds.). *Religion and Society in Early Modern England*. New York: Routledge, 1996.

Dickens, A. G. *The Counter Reformation*. University Park, PA: Pennsylvania State University Press, 1991.

Duffy, Eamon. *The Stripping of the Alters: Traditional Religion in England c.1400--c.1580*. New Haven, CT.: Yale University Press, 1994.

Englander, David, Diana Norman, Rosemary O'Day, and W. R. Owens. *Culture and Belief in Europe 1450-1600*. Malden, MA: Blackwell Publishers, 1990.

MacCulloch, Diarmaid. *The Later Reformation in England, 1547-1603*. New York: St. Martin's Press, 2001.

O'Day, Rosemary. *The Debate on the English Reformation*. New York: Routledge, 1986.

Pettegree, Andrew (ed.). *The Early Reformation in Europe*. New York: Cambridge University Press, 1993.

Rummel, Erika (ed.). *The Erasmus Reader*. Toronto: University of Toronto Press, 1995.

INDEX

Page numbers in *italics* indicate pictures.